of our
Savior
to change
lives
is a
positive,
marvelous
fact;
indeed,
the greatest
fact
of all.

NORMAN VINCENT PEALE

THE POSITIVE POWER OF JESUS CHRIST

LIVING BOOKS
Tyndale House Publishers, Inc.
Wheaton, Illinois

Living Books is a registered trademark
of Tyndale House Publishers, Inc.

Scripture quotations are from the
King James Version of the Bible
unless otherwise noted.

Living Books® edition

Library of congress catalog card number 79-67855
ISBN 0-8423-4875-1, trade paper
ISBN 0-8423-4914-6, Living Books edition
Copyright © 1980 by Norman Vincent Peale
Printed in the United States of America

11   12   13   14   15   93   92

To my wife
RUTH STAFFORD PEALE
my partner in all our ministry,
whose inspiring Christian life
has taught me much about
The Positive Power of Jesus Christ

CONTENTS

INTRODUCTION
Why This Book?

When one has published twenty-four books it would seem that is enough. And actually I had entertained no definite thought of writing another book. But then three things happened that changed my mind and resulted in this volume.

The first was that Dr. Wendell Hawley of Tyndale House Publishers wrote requesting an interview. I met him at our *Guideposts* editorial office at 747 Third Avenue in New York City. He said he hoped I would write a distinctly religious book as distinguished from the religious-motivational books which I had previously written. He seemed aware of my strong evangelical convictions and expressed the thought that a book describing the changed lives through faith in Jesus Christ which had occurred through my ministry could, perhaps, be helpful to many. Having had the feeling for a long time that I would eventually like to write such a book telling of the many persons with whom I had been involved as they experienced the saving power of the Lord, Dr.

Hawley's suggestion seemed an expression of God's guidance.

He stated that he would like the title of the book to be *The Positive Power of Jesus Christ*. At first I had trouble with this title, thinking that it might be criticized as a sort of gimmicky play on the title of my book, *The Power of Positive Thinking*. And as one who venerates and respects Jesus so profoundly, any suggestion of "using" Him was repugnant to me. However, as I thought and prayed about the matter I reminded myself that I had lived too long to be much concerned about possible criticism, and furthermore the title seemed to say something very important; namely, that the power of Jesus Christ is indeed positive and life-changing. I decided, therefore, to go with the title, believing that it showed great respect for the beloved Master who effects a positive and powerful change within us when we yield to His saving grace.

A second reason for writing this book, if I needed a reason, is that I have always witnessed to the work of Christ in my own life, in my long ministry, and in the life experience of many with whom I have either had a pastoral relationship or have communicated by books, radio, television, public speeches, or by other methods. I felt that I would like very much for my last book (if it should be that) to be a strong, clear, and loving witness to my faith in the Lord Jesus Christ and an expression of gratitude for all He has done for me, one of the least of His servants.

And, finally, I received a letter which I publish here. It is one of many letters which have come to me from time to time saying the same thing. I have never met the writer of the letter which appears below, but obviously it is a friendly and kindly suggestion which he makes. It came at just the opportune time, and not only impressed me by its sincerity and wisdom, but it also urged an action which, as I said previously, had been germinating in my mind. The letter follows:

Dear Dr. Peale,

For many years I have been receiving your literature. I have found it to be a very great help and feel that it served its purpose as a signpost pointing toward a Christian life. I just wanted you to know that God is using your work to reach the lost.

Now that I have found Christ I can understand the full meaning of your books and your monthly messages, "Creative Help for Daily Living." Life is truly worth living using these principles.

Dr. Peale, I have been thinking that possibly you have yet to write your greatest book. If you would write concerning your relationship to Jesus Christ as your Savior and the center of your being, possibly it would tie all your works together into one understandable whole.

I can see that your writings have been aimed at the greatest possible audience and I thank you for that. Had you pushed Christ rather than His principles you would have "turned off" many people. By selling His principles you have effectively unlocked the doors for others to make an effective witness for Christ. However, now, if you can put forth Christ in one book, think how it would throw light on all your previous works.

Thank you again for your part in bringing me to Christ.

In Him,
Jim McCallion

This book is my humble tribute to our Lord Jesus Christ. I wish it were more worthy, for a tribute to Him should be of exquisite quality. Yet, with all its manifest and obvious imperfections, this book is my simple of-

fering of love to our blessed Lord and Savior Jesus
Christ, who has done so much for me in life and in
whom I trust for life eternal.

Norman Vincent Peale

1

Some Early Encounters with the Power

SOMETIMES AN EVENT OCCURS IN A PERSON'S life with dramatic suddenness, and as a result that person is never the same again. The experience may penetrate so deeply into personality that it leaves a permanent impression. And that powerful effect can possibly change the individual for life.

Such an unforgettable and determinative experience happened to me when I was a very small boy. It conditioned my thinking and living for a lifetime. It happened on a cold February night in a little village in the Midwest of the United States. The snow lay deep around the white steepled church. Light gleamed through the windows, welcoming the worshipers who struggled through the drifts, stamping off snow at the door. The little church was filled to the last seat, with many standing.

It was the midwinter revival series, with evangelistic preaching every night for a two-week period. "Protracted meetings," I seem to remember they were called. The interest developed was intense, especially if the preacher, in this case my father, was well-known throughout the area as a powerful speaker motivated by a sincere faith and dedication to Jesus Christ. Since in those days there was no radio or television to compete, and, indeed, no motion picture theater, the church was the center and focal point of interest. A special series of revival meetings, long anticipated, attracted not only regular churchgoers but all others as well. Few were so irreligious as to ignore the excitement generated as the meetings progressed night after night.

I was present each night, sitting near the front with my mother and younger brother, Bob, and felt the excitement and awareness of God's presence that developed as the revival series mounted in zeal. It was a controlled emotional content, however, for my father was suspicious of the emotionalism that sometimes prevailed at such meetings and often resulted in a falling away of people converted superficially. What he wanted was in-depth life change in which not only emotion but the mind combined in a commitment bringing spiritual growth and lifelong Christian discipleship. There was in the air the excitement of great things happening, and on one particular night something great did happen.

There was a man in the community, Dave Henderson, who was a very rough, tough character. He would go on regular drunks. Nowadays he would be considered an alcoholic. His speech was very profane and he could easily be provoked into a fight. And he had a mean streak that was revealed in violent outbursts of temper. Rumor had it that he was a wife-beater, but his sweet and dignified mate never let on that he was anything but a perfect husband.

Despite everything, there was something about Dave that was likable, and my father, a "he-man" type of minister, was rather fond of him. I recall his saying, "There is something pretty fine in that man if he would only let the Lord bring it out." And Dave, in turn, liked my father. He would often come to church, sitting in a rear pew, and afterward say to Father, "I like to hear you talk, Reverend." But still he went on with his life style which most charitably could be described, to use words prevalent in those days, as wicked and evil. He was the bad man of the town.

THE MIRACLE HAPPENS

Then came this unforgettable night. The meeting opened with the congregational singing of old revival hymns.

Prayer was offered, the Scriptures read. Then Father went into his sermon. He was always tender and loving; most persuasive. He loved Jesus, and that love communicated itself impressively to the congregation. He told how great Jesus is; that the Savior can do the most wonderful things in even the worst lives. The sermon was thoughtful, intelligent; the message irrefutable in its logical presentation. And it was heightened by love. My father loved those people, and one by one he had loved them into the Kingdom.

He finished his sermon by giving the invitation to all who wanted to be saved and know the Lord, to be converted and have their lives changed, to come forward to the altar and receive the power, the power of Christ.

There was a moment of silence. Then I could almost feel the church shake a bit as a heavy man started down the aisle. Seated at the end of the pew, I looked back to see who it was. It was Dave, walking with a kind of determined air, quite unconscious of the stir he was creating. Tears were streaming down his cheeks. Even though I was a small boy, I was well aware that this man was deeply moved.

Reaching the altar, Dave knelt. Father knelt with him and, as he later told us, said to him, "Dave, you have been struggling against God, and that is no good. God wants you, my dear friend, and if you surrender to Him He will give you peace and joy and your life will be wonderful forever."

Dave said quietly, "Reverend, I want Jesus. I can't do anything with my life. I don't want to be this way anymore."

Father put his hand on the big fellow's shoulder and said, "Receive Jesus Christ who forgives all your sins and makes you now His own."

I could not hear this conversation. It was spoken in very low tones, and I report it here from memory as told to me by my father over seventy years ago. Then Dave rose and turned around to face the congregation, all of whom knew him for his bad qualities and actions. He said only, "Jesus! Thank You, Jesus!" But it was the look on his face that got me, and, indeed, everyone else. It was a look that was out of this world in its beauty. This man's countenance was transformed, illuminated. It was beautiful. It was so incredibly wonderful that tears welled up in my eyes. The feeling I had was one of wonderment, astonishment. How could this be? Surely this wasn't happening to *this* man! And just what was happening? The answer is that the positive power of Jesus Christ was happening. A man was being changed.

And Dave was changed. Some people said it wouldn't last. But it did last. From that moment this man was totally different. He broke instantly with all his bad habits. He became a good, honorable, upright man of God. Literally he became a saint, a rugged, loving saint. And if I were called upon to name the best men, the most Christlike men I have ever known, Dave Henderson would be right up there at the top of the list.

But still, even though I was only a small boy, I was confused. How could this be—a man walks into a church one sort of man and leaves the church totally different? "What happened, Father?" I asked. "What happened to Dave in that one minute of time?"

Father smiled. "It's wonderful, Norman; it's all very wonderful. The power happened to him. He received the power—the positive power of Jesus Christ. He is a new man in Christ." I can recall to this day my father repeating that glorious line from Scripture: "If any man be in Christ, he is a new creature: old things are passed away; behold, all things are become new."[1] Then Father added, "The fact that Jesus Christ can do this to people made me a preacher."

And, I might add, it made me a preacher also.

THE BLESSING

So the years passed and Dave kept the faith. He walked among men as a man of God. He was beloved, even venerated. He was a blessing to everyone he met. His big head was finally crowned with snowy white hair. Love and kindness were written on his rugged countenance. Then he became ill and I received word that the end was near. I immediately went from my home in New York back to the little town where he lived to see him once more. He lay in bed, his white hair against the pillow. His giant form was now emaciated. His big hand, now so thin, was white against the sheet, and the blue veins showed clearly. We talked of the old times, particularly of my father. "Greatest man I ever knew," said Dave. "He led me to Christ. And what greater thing can one man do for another?"

Then I asked Dave to pray for me. I knelt by the side of his bed and could feel his hand reaching for me. Presently it rested on my head. I cannot now recall just what he said and I've never before written this story. I only know that this was a sacred experience. I felt cleansed and blessed. I felt the Holy Presence. It was one of the few deepest and most beautiful spiritual experiences of life.

1. 2 Corinthians 5:17

I stood to say good-bye and we both knew it was the last good-bye until we should meet in Heaven. My mind flashed back to that night so long ago, and apparently his did, too, for he said, "You were with me the night I was reborn, Norman. I've always loved you."

"And I you, Dave," I said. "You will live in my heart always."

And so we parted for a while.

THE EVANGELISTIC CHURCH

This experience of the power enthralled me, and the emotion has lasted for a lifetime. I realized that only Jesus Christ can change weak persons into strong people. Only Jesus Christ can change evil human nature into good men and women. I was fascinated with the power, with the wonder-working power that produces changed lives, or, as I call it for the purposes of this book, the positive power of Jesus Christ. Indeed, it has to be the greatest power in the world, because it alone can change a human being, the most complicated, even perverse, of all entities. I have seen it gloriously at work in the lives of so many, some of whom I want to tell you about in this book.

I count myself fortunate to have been young in an era when there was a strong evangelistic motivation in our country. The church was dedicated to "soul winning," as the process was then called. And great emphasis was laid upon bringing young boys and girls to Christ. Preaching was directed to that end. Sunday schools had what they called "Decision Days" and parents were never happier than when their children found the Lord.

It was a beautiful time in America. It was a religious

country, genuinely so. A few writers like Sinclair Lewis and others tried to depict it as hypocritical. Undoubtedly there were some phonies. Indeed, I knew a few myself. But they were the exception rather than the rule. We were brought up to have ideals and principles, to be clean, decent, honest. Of course we were not all that perfect, but one thing is sure: we were taught to love God, to love Jesus, to love our country, to love our fellowmen. And we had a happy time. It was glorious to be young in America between the turn of the century and the twenties. That was before the church started playing down personal commitment and before the moral principles that made the nation strong and great began to be eroded. That was before prayer and Bible reading were taken out of the public schools, and before pornography became a big industry to corrupt boys and girls and pour filthy dollars into the pockets of greedy men who would debauch a nation to make a fast buck.

But God is never set aside. He alone remains. Now, happily, there is a new spiritual movement sweeping the country in the form of small spiritual groups everywhere. Once again thousands of churches are preaching and teaching the power of Christ to change lives, to bring people to peace and joy in themselves and in their families.

It was really wonderful in those earlier days how Christian parents knew instinctively, as the result of the positive power of Jesus Christ, how to deal with children. And this is a skill that we would do well to relearn. I recall once when we lived in Greenville, Ohio, and I was an adolescent that I could not sleep and was tossing restlessly. My mother came in, sat on my bed, and asked what the matter was. I was reluctant to tell her what was on my mind, but she was the kind of mother to whom a kid could talk and I blurted out, "I have bad thoughts." My mother was smart enough to know that this should be handled by my father, so she said she loved me and left the room.

BAD THOUGHTS ARE HEALED

Later I was awakened by my father sitting on my bed. "About those bad thoughts," he began directly, "girls?" I nodded shamefacedly. "They are natural. We all have had them."

"You?" I said. "You have had bad thoughts?"

"Sure. Every real boy does."

My father had been a medical doctor before becoming a minister. Indeed, I could never quite figure where the medical doctor left off and the minister began. He proceeded to give me a medical description of the "bad thought" problem, then concluded the conversation by quoting an old saying: "'You cannot prevent birds from flying over your head, but you can keep them from building nests in your hair.' It is natural for bad thoughts to come to mind. But if your mind, acting as a judge, repels them, you are stronger thereby and should in no sense feel guilty. In fact, you have gained a moral victory. And," he added, "Jesus is there to help you."

Always my mother and father made us realize that Jesus was ever there to help. And other mothers and fathers were doing the same. So powerful was this Christ-centered influence that as I think back to all the boys and girls I knew in my youth, the great majority, perhaps as many as 90 percent of them, turned out to be people of the finest character. Some had spent time, perhaps, in the "far country,"[2] but they returned, as the old parable of the prodigal son has it, to the father's house. The positive power of Jesus Christ works with kids if they have parents who believe it, who have experienced it, and who know how to use it with their children.

One thing is sure; my parents knew how. A case in point is the day my father drove me to college. As he prepared to leave after getting me settled in my room in the Phi Gamma Delta fraternity house, he said, "Norman, you have now left home for the first time. Perhaps, aside from vacations, you may never live in your old home again. Your mother and I have tried to have a Christian home. We believe it has had an influence on you. But now you are in a new world, a college world. I believe in you, that you will live straight. I hope you won't get mixed up with women or liquor or whatever. But if you get into any kind of trouble I don't want you to lie to me. Level with me and I'll try my best to get you out of it by getting the problem, whatever it is, solved." He paused; his lip trembled, and he sort of punched me in the chest. "Stick to Jesus. He will always help you." Whereupon without another word he walked to his car, rounded the corner and, with a wave of his hand, was gone. I stood there, already homesick, but never to forget that regular guy, that sturdy Christian father, always man-to-man with his son and never forgetting Jesus.

2. Luke 15:13

CURE OF INFERIORITY COMPLEX

A reason for writing this book, *The Positive Power of Jesus Christ*, is that while growing up, my brothers, Robert and Leonard, and I were always exposed to its operation. We saw it work in the life experience of countless people who were affected by the Christian ministry of our father and mother. And in the crisis times in our own lives it was invoked by our parents, who truly believed, and logically so, that faith in Jesus Christ could bring a right outcome out of any situation.

Some time after the bad thought episode my father applied the positive power of Jesus Christ to another of my problems, perhaps the most difficult problem I ever faced as a youth: namely, my horrible inferiority complex. I was shy, reticent, shrinking, filled with self-doubt. In fact, I lived like a scared rabbit. I was *bashful*. This word, not used much in later years, was a very descriptive word, meaning, as it does, abashed. I constantly told myself that I had no brains, no ability; that I didn't amount to anything and never would. I lived in a miserable world of self-depreciation. I then became aware that people were agreeing with me, for it is a fact that others will unconsciously take you at your own self-appraisal. At any rate, I was a pretty wretched victim of the inferiority complex.

One summer Sunday afternoon my father said he wanted to call on a family of his church who lived a couple of miles out of town in the country at Greenville, Ohio, and he asked me to accompany him. We went on foot, our little fox terrier, Tip, running along with us. It was a rich countryside we traveled—Darke County, Ohio—and we passed prosperous-looking farms and waved to the people, as of course we knew them all. I recall that one family persuaded us to stop for a drink of cold lemonade, it being a warm day, and then the farmer's wife served us a heaping dish of homemade vanilla ice cream with cookies. I have eaten ice cream all around the world, but this homemade dish remains in memory over all these years as the most delectable— unforgettable.

We reached the family my father wanted to visit. There was some kind of trouble to which he brought his caring spirit and practical skills. Then we started home and he got me to talking about myself. I unloaded my problem about my inferiority feelings, which had been discussed with him on previous occasions.

My father's medical experience as a doctor and his genius as a pastor made him an acute and competent curer of souls. His perception that abnormal guilt from the bad thoughts or wrong thinking about personality traits could be harmful made him adept in dealing with my inferiority feelings. Indeed, it was this religio-medical characteristic of my father that was influential in my own founding, years later, with the famous psychiatrist Dr. Smiley Blanton, of the American Foundation of Religion and Psychiatry, now called the Institutes of Religion and Health.

Finally we came to a place where several trees had been cut down, and we sat on convenient stumps. Father described the mechanism of inferiority and self-doubt feelings in a manner that would do credit to a modern psychiatrist. He stated that scientific treatment could probably cure me, but that such treatment was not available in our little village, and besides, it was quite expensive.

"But," he continued, "there is a Doctor right here who can cure any disease of the mental and emotional life. He has a rare and amazing power to correct our unhealthy thought patterns. And He can heal the sensitive self-centeredness that lies at the root of inferiority-inadequacy feelings." Long afterward when I told Dr. Blanton about this treatment he said admiringly, "Your father was a genius in his insights."

Finally Father said, "Norman, are you willing to let this great Doctor, Jesus Christ, treat you for that inferiority complex? If you will let Jesus take charge of your mind, indeed your whole life, you can be freed of this misery which, if it continues, can destroy your effectiveness." I was profoundly impressed and said I would give my life into the hands of Jesus. Father told me to kneel down by the stump and he, too, knelt. I remember that Tip came up and licked my ear, then sat beside me. Father then committed me to Christ in a moving prayer. He then asked me to tell Jesus that I was giving myself into His hands and letting go, by an act of affirmation, all my inferiority feelings. As we walked home in the gathering twilight I felt a strange sense of peace and happiness, as though I was really on top of my problems. While I had another bout with this trouble during college days later on, the same remedy was again applied, with the result that this self-defeating thought pattern was healed through the positive power of Jesus Christ.

NOT ALWAYS INSTANT CHANGE
Not everyone, of course, is instantly changed or healed. Sometimes the change or healing is long coming. God answers prayer perhaps in three ways: "Yes," "No," or "Wait awhile." That was true of my struggle with self-doubt. One day in college a professor took me to task in a rather forthright manner, asserting that I "disgusted"

him, for, so said he, "you know this material but you are so self-conscious that you are unable to express yourself. Why don't you get over this inferiority and be a man?"

This angered me and I left his office vowing to come back and beat him up and resign from the college. This, however, I did not carry out; he stood well over six feet and outweighed me by forty pounds. And I knew he was right. Standing on the steps of the main college building, I determined to get over this trouble then and there for good. My mind returned to the prayer by the stump, and once again I took my problem up with Jesus Christ, humbly asking Him please to give me His power over my self-defeat. He did, and at that moment power came into my life.

These early personal encounters with the positive power of Jesus Christ led me to the conclusion that if the power could work successfully in my life, perhaps I could convince others that it might work similarly for them.

Early on in my ministry I had a curious experience which caused me to believe that, perhaps through my personal witness to Christ's healing power, I might be able to draw many to Him. I had just completed my first year in the seminary, studying to be a minister, and had returned home to Findlay, Ohio, for the summer. At that time my father was superintendent over some seventy-five churches in the area, and one of them, a country church, was without a minister for the following Sunday, the pastor being ill. Would I be the preacher in his stead?

Along about Saturday I was sitting on the porch with Mother and Father and asked if they would listen to me read the sermon I intended to give the next day. It was

27

a very complex theological discourse, full of big words and impressive phrases. "You know," said Mother, "you are going to speak to farmers, the finest people on earth, but most of them not too well educated." Father was more direct. "I suggest," he said, "that you burn up that manuscript. Just go there tomorrow and talk simply to those good people. Love them and tell them what you know about Jesus. Tell them how He has helped you personally."

Somewhat deflated, I went next day to the church, which stood at the corner of two white, dusty roads. All around were cornfields, the corn being "knee high by the fourth of July," as the old saying goes. I felt inadequately prepared. The church was full, the people all in their Sunday best. I rose to speak and began telling of the various times in my life when Jesus had helped me. I told all about the inferiority problem and talked simply and out of my heart about the power of Christ in one's life. I noticed that a deep stillness fell upon the crowded church, so still I could hear the buzzing of a bee that had flown in the window in the summer air.

The sermon was quite short, and following it I was invited by a nice farmer's wife to their home for Sunday dinner. I sat with the men on the verandah while the womenfolk prepared dinner. The tantalizing aroma of frying chicken wafted to our nostrils as we talked. The farmer, a huge man, sat down in a rocking chair beside me. "You know, son," he said, "you've got a powerful lot to learn about preaching."

"Yes, sir, I know that for a fact."

"But you're right about one thing. I've had that same inferiority trouble you had. I didn't believe in myself. But I found Jesus and believed in Him, and He made me believe I could do things. I've loved Jesus ever since.

So just stick to Jesus and tell people about His power."

Years later I wrote a book and called it *The Power of Positive Thinking*. It came out of my own struggles to find myself. And then I remembered that fine old Midwest farmer whom Jesus also helped to find himself. Now here I am writing a book which also goes back to my early encounters with the power, the amazing grace of Jesus. And I call the book *The Positive Power of Jesus Christ* because the power of our Savior to change lives is a positive, marvelous fact; indeed, the greatest fact of all.

2

Personal
Experience
of the Power

WHILE IN THIS BOOK WE ARE DEALING primarily with the fascinating accounts of persons who have experienced the positive power of Jesus Christ, I shall from time to time introduce references to my own personal encounters with that power. Being involved in the spiritual experiences of others necessarily has resulted in a deepening of my own pilgrimage with God.

Mine has been a cumulative growth in the spirit. I have had not one but several experiences of deeper commitment. Not once but more than once have I committed my life to Christ. And each succeeding experience became life-changing in greater depth, profounder meaning, and inspiring spiritual growth. Each experience of the grace of God through Christ has had for me its own validity, its own wonderment, its own deepening of joy and peace.

Not very long after I first saw the positive power of Jesus Christ in action, as related in chapter one, our family moved to Cincinnati, Ohio. Again my father had a series of revival meetings. It had not occurred to me that I needed "saving," for was I not a minister's son and, therefore, by birth and inheritance a Christian? I had no sins that I knew of and was living the carefree, normal life of a good boy from a good home. My brother and I had our mischievous streaks and were quite vigorous kids, but as to requiring salvation, that was not for us.

Mother taught a Sunday school class for boys. She was a natural-born and highly gifted communicator. Besides, she knew boys very well and what would appeal to them. So her Sunday school talks were a bit about the Cincinnati Reds and a lot about the greatness of Jesus. She described His boyhood, young manhood and, finally, how He went about doing good and helping people. She described graphically how He "set his face to go to Jerusalem,"[1] and the manly courage that was required to go to the Cross for our salvation.

Her description of His endurance of suffering and pain as He carried the Cross really reached us, and we were thrilled and impressed when Pilate exclaimed, "*Ecce homo!*" (Behold the man!).[2] Mother made it read, "What a man!" So when she asked Bob and me to follow Him, we declared, "For now and always." At the same time she got over to us that there was sin in us from our belonging to the human race and that only the blood of Christ could wash it out and protect us from any more of it. We stood with others at the altar of the church, hand in hand, looking up at our father and publicly confessing Christ. My mother told me years later that Bob and I came to her that night and said we felt peace and joy in our hearts.

This was a normal and healthy development of boys under the guidance of committed Christian parents. I lived on happily following Christ in my own boyish way until in adolescence I began to experience the conflicts and self-defeatism described in the first chapter. It was then that I had to seek the deeper power flow of faith in Christ, and in so doing I found what I call the positive power of Jesus Christ in full measure. Of course this was accomplished by complete acceptance of Jesus Christ as Lord and Savior, by the remission of sin and the way of salvation as outlined in the New Testament. I found that by accepting and living the gospel as described in the New Testament, one found the power to live the Christlike life in victory.

When I made the decision to become a minister, it

1. Luke 9:51   2. John 19:5

was because I felt a definite calling to witness to Christ in my own life and to proclaim my belief that faith in Him is the sure way to creative living. I became a student in the School of Theology of Boston University. There I got the impression, rightly or wrongly, that personal life-changing was taking second place to what was considered a more important preachment—that of social change. I believed in social justice and the need for the church to point the way. I believed that changed people change the world. I also believed that personal life change was the primary work of Christ. Accordingly, in my first church in Berkeley, Rhode Island, I witnessed, preached, and taught both publicly and one-to-one that the positive power of Jesus Christ was available to give new life to anyone who would accept the Savior and live His way of life. Sunday after Sunday I proclaimed this message and repeated this promise. The church began to fill up with people out of the cotton-mill-working population of the area. These people knew at first hand the problems of industrialization, and there had been a lengthy strike in which I backed in every possible way the cause of the workers. We made considerable progress in that area.

HE LOST HIS INNER HELL
But there still persisted the old human problems of immorality, of ill will and contention, of drunkenness, dishonesty, sexual depravity and every form of evil, with the resulting unhappiness of human beings. I declared and witnessed to the fact that always in Christ is new life, forgiveness, peace, joy, and victory for anyone who will believe. One Sunday night, seated in the pulpit, I saw through an open window a man approaching

the church who had the reputation of being, as one person described him, "a devil full of hate." I had encountered him only casually and had never seen this side of the man. Later I learned that he had an almost ungovernable temper; indeed, so violent that it had cost him several jobs, though he was well trained and a competent person otherwise.

In the sermon, which had, of course, been previously prepared, I told of instances where individuals plagued with various weaknesses turned them over to Christ and were delivered of them. Then, without any planning beforehand and with no thought of this man, I said, "If you want to overcome a weakness, however defeating it may be, if you will come forward to the altar, confess your sinfulness, and ask humbly for the grace of God, you can be free of your weakness."

Astonishingly, several persons came forward, including the man with all the hate. He knelt and looked up at me. "I've got a rotten disposition," he admitted. "Do you mean what you said? I want to get changed. Will Christ change me?" Thus he laid it on the line. Since I am a believer and no doubter at all in these promises, I replied, "He not only will, but has already done so, because the very act of coming forward proves you to be a believer. 'According to your faith be it unto you.'[3] The devil has come out of you."

His face showed his surprise. I prayed and thanked God for the new disposition which had just been given this man. Leaving the church that summer night, I was literally walking on air, so excited I could hardly endure the feeling. I had no doubt at all about the man, for everyone in that service had definitely felt the positive

3. Matthew 9:29

power of Jesus Christ. The man wanted deliverance; he was fed up with what he was; he heard the gospel, he believed, and he was saved from the hell of himself. And he remained a controlled man, experiencing deep inner peace until the day he died and went on to eternal life.

I was told later, when I informed other ministers of this incident, that I had not handled the matter at all correctly—that the man's faith would have been greatly shaken had it not worked out as I promised. It was further stated that I should have referred him to a psychiatrist who would have found the roots of his trouble in frustrated childhood. But actually the man had no faith to be shaken. It was my positive assertion that transmitted faith to him. My belief became his belief, and his belief turned into new life. This experience taught me that the convinced proclamation of belief in Christ's power to save brings about astonishing changes in people's lives.

The conclusion is that belief in God, in Jesus, and in the Holy Spirit is the basic element in life-changing. This has been true in my own life as well as in the lives of others. Learn to believe, to "fight the good fight of faith,"[4] and you become the beneficiary of the grace of God and have power over all your weaknesses. Accordingly, my aim has always been to be a true believer in the Lord, to be a person of ever-deepening faith. That faith and belief have deepened with every passing year, for which I am profoundly thankful.

It has been my purpose through the years to proclaim this power of belief in all my books. One book was at first titled *The Power of Faith*. But my desire was to reach

4. 1 Timothy 6:12

the unchurched people of the nation, and I reluctantly decided that such a title would scarcely interest any but committed religious persons. My publisher and good friend, Myron Boardman, noticed a repetitive phrase in the text and called my attention to the use of it. It was "the power of positive thinking." "That," said Myron, "is saying the same thing, really, and is perhaps a title that would have greater appeal to those outside the church whom you wish to reach." I saw the reasonableness of this suggestion and gave that title to the book.

THE POWER STARTED FLOWING

The Power of Positive Thinking was very successful as a publication, selling millions of copies, and the vast correspondence from readers indicated that God used it to change thousands of lives and to bring them to Christ. Here follows one letter out of the thousands that came and keep coming:

Dear Dr. Peale:

For twenty-five years I had been progressing from a heavy drinker to a hopeless alcoholic. I had lost position after position, had been locked up for common drunkenness, been confined in alcoholic wards, spent many weeks in mental wards in various hospitals—not that I was mentally unbalanced in the usual sense, but because these were the places where alcoholics were confined while being given treatment.

For years I was completely out of touch with my mother, sisters and brother. My marriage, never a happy one, dissolved. At one time I had owned two portrait studios—I am a photographer—and these, of course, I lost. I spent a year and a half a hopeless drunk on skid row in Philadelphia.

I heard of Alcoholics Anonymous and attended some meetings. I tried to work the program, but had too many reservations. I thought negatively on everything. But the teachings of AA beat against the sides of my head and, I found out later, quite a bit filtered through and remained.

Then the first good thing that had come my way in years occurred. I met a fine woman in the Jacksonville, Florida, AA and a year later we were married. However, not long afterward we both began drinking again and things went from bad to worse.

I took to my bed with a bottle—my usual routine when a difficult problem arose—and passed out. My wife Florence, to pass the time, went downtown to the library. Somehow she stumbled across a book of yours, *The Power of Positive Thinking*, glanced through it and, as she later told me, rushed home and put it on my night table. Whenever I came to in my drinking bouts, I usually liked to read something—anything—as it seemed to calm me down.

So I reached out and picked up this library book and began reading it. At first, of course, none of it made much sense to me due to my mental condition. I remember closing it and placing it once more on the table, thinking I would look at it another time. But a phrase I read when I had opened it at random seemed to be making its way through my muddled thoughts. "If God is with me, who can be against me?"[5] I tried visualizing Him there beside me and immediately felt assured and stronger. I then picked up the book again and commenced reading from the beginning, feeling better as I went along.

During the next few days, reading a little each day, I could feel a resolve within myself becoming stronger and stronger to regain and keep my sobriety.

My wife and I celebrated our fourth anniversary the other day—four years without a drink. We don't have

5. Romans 8:31, paraphrased

too much in the way of material, worldly goods, but we are very happy. I manage a portrait studio and photograph mostly children. We have nice clothes, own our own car, attend the Episcopal Church, and hope to build our own home next year. It all happened through the power of Jesus Christ working in us.

Some critics have read into the title, *The Power of Positive Thinking*, an emphasis on material success. They failed to study the text itself, which outlines the power of belief which I had learned in my own spiritual pilgrimage. From my personal relationship with Jesus Christ I knew that the promise, "You shall receive power when the Holy Spirit has come upon you,"[6] is absolutely valid. It is belief—not belief in yourself—but belief in Jesus Christ that gives the power. If you have faith even as a grain of mustard seed, and do not doubt, you can say to whatever big mountain of failure or difficulty, "Be you gone," and it will go. The end result is that nothing will be impossible.[7] I believe that promise, really believe it, and taught it to others, like the man mentioned earlier in this chapter, and as a result I have witnessed and am continuing to witness tremendous demonstrations of the positive power of Jesus Christ. This faith, this belief, became and remains the greatest thing in my life, and, through my sharing it, others have found the faith. Praise the Lord!

WORK UNDERSTOOD

Of course it means much to an author to have his work understood. However, in the nature of things he must not be surprised at misunderstanding, and certainly he

6. Acts 1:8, RSV   7. Matthew 17:20, paraphrased

40

should not let it deflect him from his conscientious objectives. Still, being human, an author is encouraged when persons who have misunderstood his beliefs come to an understanding by finding spiritual help from his writings.

Following is a letter similar to many I have received in which the writer is kind enough to say that, whereas he once had his doubts, he now understands that over the years we have indeed been seeking to lead people to the Lord:

> Dear Dr. Peale:
>
> I just finished reading a book you wrote 30 years ago, *A Guide to Confident Living* (© 1948), and wanted to tell you how much it meant to me.
>
> I work for Asbury Theological Seminary as Director of Deferred Giving and Bequests and as Staff Legal Counsel. In those roles, I travel quite a bit, and I'm sure I don't need to recount to you the tortures of lengthy airport waits. So I try to always have a book with me, to fill the space. Recently, on the way out the door, heading for Bluegrass Airport, I grabbed this book from a shelf in my office. I was looking for something that might speak to my needs.
>
> Because of burdens which have come my way in recent months, there was no joy; only reasons to find fault with everyone and everything. Believe me, that's no way to live—much less spread the love of Christ in the land! Somehow, all that I knew and all I had experienced was not sufficient for the day.
>
> When I came to the chapter on "How to Achieve a Calm Center for Your Life," I knew you were writing to me.
>
> And the thought—"Having done all—stand"[8]—Wow—I was on my way.
>
> The transformation of the mind by Christ—positive

8. Ephesians 6:13

thoughts rather than negative—I believe now it can be accomplished.

I've let go and allowed God to lift me to a plane above my circumstances. In fact, for the first time ever, I can say—"God, I am thankful *for* my trials, because they have brought me closer to You."

I have a confession to make. This was the first book of yours I have read. The reason: I had the notion that you were preaching things like self-help (without God), humanism, success motivation, etc.—of which I was skeptical. Well, please forgive me. You have captured the very essence of the Christian message and made it so very *practical* that you can't misunderstand it. And isn't that the whole task of every Christian—to bring Christ to the people in a meaningful way?

One other thing—Thank you for using examples of business and professional people. So much of today's Christian literature is good, but there isn't much written which understands the plight of the man out in the business world in a realistic way. But your ministry— situated as it is—has put you in a unique position to know the particular trials and problems of that segment.

May God bless you.

Sincerely,
Richard Edwards

P.S. We enjoy so much your Sunday morning telecast and *Guideposts* each month.

THE POWER IS ALWAYS AT WORK

During all of my adult life I have been in public speaking—not alone in the church, but in various kinds of public meetings such as national business conventions, sales rallies, community gatherings, and the like. In connection with this activity I have had some unforgettable experiences. One day four other speakers shared the platform with me in a huge sports arena type of auditorium near the Minneapolis airport. Nearly 18,000 persons filled the arena to overcapacity for what the promoters called a Positive Mental Attitude Rally.

Going along routinely in my speech doing the best I could, all of a sudden something happened to me. It was as if time stood still; a deep hush settled over the big crowd. The people seemed silhouetted in sharp, clear light. Everyone appeared immobile and frozen into place, and all eyes seemed to bore straight into me. They seemed to have a pleading air, as if each one was saying, "Please, please say something to me, something that will help me. Give me real answers, not words— answers that really answer."

The spell lasted but a minute, perhaps hardly even that. Maybe it was only a fraction of a second. But I was shaken by those faces, most of them young people, but old as well as young mutely demanding something, pleading for a deep, meaningful something that would help them. The thing that disturbed me was whether I was in any sense able to lead them to what they wanted. Was I only talking, simply making a speech, then moving on to another talk, another speech, and more talk elsewhere? I will, I think, forever recall that fraction of a moment as I stood before that vast audience, hand raised in a gesture, finger pointing, receiving back the reflection of those eyes, those deep, searching eyes! They were beautiful eyes, for people are beautiful in their deeper moments, and I loved them all. Was I helping them to find what they wanted, those people whose eyes searched mine?

Actually, what did they want? Did they themselves know what they were reaching for? Why did 18,000 persons pay good money to hear five speakers at a motivational gathering on that October day? The question is a searching one, an old, human, and universal inquiry:

what do people want? What do you and I want in this fleeting life during our short tenure upon this little island in space?

That we do want something, deeply want something, is certain. This deep, basic desire, regardless of what name you may apply to it, is very real. This vague yet utterly fundamental yearning that bugs us and eats at us all our lives is resolutely insistent. For long days, even months, or perhaps even years, it may be quiescent and dormant. And just when you think it no longer exists or is at all active, the agitation begins again, perhaps even stronger than ever before. That strong wanting never dies, nor even weakens. In one form or other, insistent and demanding, it still reaches for something and will not be denied.

But what is it that people want? What do you want; what do I want? Actually, the basic problem should be described in other terms. To determine specifically what the heart of an individual craves would be only to satisfy a philosophical curiosity. The main problem is that the individual wants to find himself, somewhere and somehow to know his identity, for in so doing he will find that which he wants. The basic desire is inextricably related to the fundamentals of personality. When you find what you want, then in a profound sense you have found your own self. And in finding yourself you come upon that which you truly desire.

On that October day I caught myself saying to this vast crowd of 18,000 seeking souls, "I can only tell you how I found what I deeply wanted. I decided to be a true follower of the way of life set forth in the Bible by Jesus Christ. I determined to do everything His way. It wasn't all that easy, but the more sincerely I tried, the better I did with my life. And I felt Him close and very real, helping me over the rough spots. In finding Jesus Christ personally in this way, I found myself, and in finding myself found what I really wanted from life."

Then I went on with my speech on the subject, "Why Positive Thinkers Get Positive Results," a motivational talk designed to stimulate listeners to more effective performance. It was not a sermon, although the spiritual note was clear and distinct.

Finishing the speech, I left the platform and headed for a car waiting to take me to the airport. But I was overtaken by a young woman. "Oh, please, wait. I must speak to you," she cried. I saw that she was weeping. Struggling to control herself, she managed to say, "As I sat in that audience just inside the door from the stage, which explains how I could get out so fast to catch you, I was completely despondent. My life has been a failure. My marriage has broken up. I went into business, into sales work, and here again I have failed."

By this time she was more composed and I noticed a kind of radiance reflected on her face, at least that is how it appeared to me—sort of like sunshine coming through rain. "I haven't known what I wanted," she said. "My heart and mind were empty. I wanted something meaningful that would change my error-and-failure life pattern and give me some happiness. Then when you gave that brief but obviously sincere witness about your own finding of yourself through commitment to our Lord Jesus Christ, something flashed through my mind like a bright light. 'This is it,' I said to myself; 'this is it.' Right then and there, with all my heart, I gave my life into the hands of the Lord. I just wanted you to know that you reached one mixed-up, unhappy person. But I'm different now, very different. I have found me at last by finding Him."

So saying, she turned and went back into the auditorium. As the car took me to the airport I wondered how many more out of that 18,000-person audience might have felt the Lord through that humble witness. One never knows how far a spiritual witness may carry. But I know that the Lord, for some reason known to Him, gave me this curious experience of people unconsciously reaching for something. They seemed to be reaching for a vague something, but if they only knew it they were reaching for a real vital Person; indeed, a Savior. Basically, He is what America wants, what the world wants. Jesus came to give life, abundant life, enough to satisfy anyone.

Such experiences as the foregoing, and they have been many in number, have taught me always to witness; never to let an opportunity go by to relate Jesus Christ to people. This of course must be done rightly and in good order, and never in a manner to turn people off. It must be done graciously, lovingly, with total absence of cant or piosity. It must be done with naturalness, as though it were an integral part of life, as indeed it is. It was said of Jesus that He was "full of grace and truth,"[9] which seems to indicate that He has the truth, the right way about everything. This fact, however, must be transmitted graciously and always in a manner to attract rather than to repel. And wherever Jesus is so presented, people find themselves loving Him, believing in Him, going for Him.

ON A GARDEN BENCH IN ENGLAND
There was an immensely popular television program some years ago, hosted by Ralph Edwards, called "This

9. John 1:14

Is Your Life." Each featured guest was maneuvered onto the show by friendly subterfuge, not realizing beforehand that he or she was the subject of that particular program. As a result, the guest could have no possible opportunity for preparation. I was startled, therefore, when Ralph Edwards confronted me with a question on this show, with an audience of millions watching. "What," he asked, "was your greatest experience in life?" But I knew the answer to that question without the necessity for any rehearsal. "It happened," I replied, "on a bench in a garden in England."

The story begins actually when I was the youthful pastor of the University (Avenue) Methodist Church in Syracuse, New York, as it was then styled, before the denominational name was changed to United Methodist as it is currently known. I had finished a little over five exciting years of service in this church when I received a call to become minister of the First Methodist Church in Los Angeles, then considered one of the largest churches numerically, if not the largest, in the denomination. At the same time I received a call to the Marble Collegiate Church at Fifth Avenue and 29th Street in New York City. The latter church was at a low ebb in its long and distinguished history dating from 1628. Indeed, it is the oldest Protestant church in the United States, having a continuous ministry from the date of its establishment. Dr. Daniel A. Poling, the former minister, had been gone from the church for nearly three years, and the membership had been reduced to approximately 500 persons. The attendance at morning and evening services had dwindled to about 200 people at each service, this in a large sanctuary with a balcony on three sides which was never occupied.

In making a decision between a huge, going church

and an almost moribund one, I discovered that one can, for a fact, get a definite answer through prayer, and a right decision as well, if one is willing to accept God's answer to his prayers. After some thirty days of indecision regarding these two churches, I came home for lunch one day and began going over the problem for possibly the hundredth time. My wife Ruth, a practical woman with strong and certain faith, declared that the time had come for an uninterrupted prayer session with the definite objective of reaching a decision. She insisted, therefore, that we both continue to pray until the answer came, and to do so then and there. I agreed and we must have prayed for two or three hours; indeed, we lost track of time.

Finally I asked, "Did you get an answer?"

"Yes, I did," replied Ruth.

"What is the answer?" I queried.

"I won't tell you," she replied, "because it must be your answer. While I am your wife and your partner, you are the minister. The answer must be yours and yours alone. And did you get an answer in your prayer?"

"Yes," I nodded, "I have an answer, and I feel definitely and certainly that it is from God."

"And what answer did you get?"

"To go to New York and to decline the invitation to Los Angeles."

"That is precisely the answer that came to me. Why not go to the telephone now and tell the man in New York that we accept the call to Marble Collegiate Church."

I did. Immediately upon reaching the chairman of the Pulpit Committee and giving him my decision an overwhelming feeling of peace flooded my mind and with it the positive assurance that the right decision had been made. There was not the slightest sense of doubt. And I may add that I have felt right about it ever since; even now, nearly half a century later. In this experience I discovered with certainty that God's guidance is obtainable through prayer if one is willing to put himself completely under the will of God.

So it was that Ruth and I came to Marble Collegiate Church, a stately and beautiful old edifice erected in 1854, when Fifth Avenue was an unpaved dirt road leading into the rural area north of 14th Street. But the church had declined in every way, and to add to our problems, the country was in the depths of the worst financial and economic depression in history. Thousands walked the streets looking futilely for jobs. Long bread lines formed before soup kitchens. Factories were shut down. Every day more and more employees were discharged by business concerns desperately trying to keep going. Business closings were a daily occurrence. It was a strange, sad, gloomy time.

Naturally, these conditions adversely affected the church, especially financially. However, there was still opportunity in the situation. "Man's extremity is God's opportunity," so it has been said, and so it proved in those tragic days of the early 1930s. People were discouraged, depressed, hopeless, and haunted by fear. To the handful who came to worship in the almost empty church, I began to stress a positive faith that God loved them and would help them no matter how tough things were. In Christ's name I assured people that by a positive and truly believing faith a new day would dawn, and that with the Lord's help each one could begin again.

As a result of this type of preaching, which was enthusiastic, always soundly based on God's Word and filled with faith, people began to respond and gradually to work out of their gloomy thinking. The congregation began to grow, but very, very slowly, and the going was hard. Perhaps for everyone it was the most difficult period of this sort the country had ever experienced, and it was most keenly felt in New York City, the financial center of the nation.

Indeed, progress in the church came so slowly that I began myself to become discouraged, and that discouragement either caused or was caused by an accompanying stress and tension. Then came the first summer vacation period, and Ruth and I went to the Lake District of England and settled down at the Station Hotel in the charming town of Keswick. Here was to occur perhaps the supreme spiritual experience of our lives.

We tried to relax and enjoy ourselves, and Ruth was able to accomplish that quite successfully, she being by nature more optimistic. But I was disconsolate, low in spirit, plagued by self-doubt. We took long walks among the beautiful streams and hills of one of the world's loveliest areas. We visited the literary shrines with which this section abounds—the homes of Wordsworth, Ruskin, and other greats of English literature. But to no avail for me. The gloom of New York and the desolate state of the church had pervasively seeped into my mind and discolored it. Despite my enthusiastic preaching back in New York, I was myself pretty low on optimism.

The hotel was situated in a magnificent English garden with clipped hedgerows and formal flower beds and well-placed benches from which you could look out at the glorious hills roundabout. We walked daily in this garden and in particular sat on one bench at the far end.

There I would pour my woes into the ears of my loving and patient young wife.

But one day as we were seated together on that bench she said, "Norman, you are my husband, but you are also my pastor. I sit in church and listen to you preach the gospel of Christ with love and enthusiasm. But to hear you talk now, I wonder if you actually have any faith at all. God called you to New York. He wants you to do His work, and He will stand by you and help you. He never promised that you could have it easy, and it is out of struggle that victory comes." Thus she delivered a sound lecture and revealed me quite clearly to myself. And the revelation was not at all pleasant.

"What you need to do," she continued, "is to surrender your church, your problems, your entire self to Christ. You have done this before, but do it again now, and perhaps even in greater depth. As you do this, I promise you will receive peace, joy, new energy, and a quality of enthusiasm that will never run down. And," she added forcefully, "you are going to sit right here on this bench until you make that surrender." My wife can be very sweet and gentle but, believe me, she can also be firm, unyielding, and very tough. And she was now fully in the latter state. Then she began to pray for me and really lifted me and herself and all of our problems up to God. Then she said, "Surrender yourself and everything to Christ. Do it again, even as you have done it before."

"Dear Lord Jesus," I prayed, "I cannot handle my life. I need help. I need You. I hereby with all my heart surrender my mind, my soul, my life to You. Use me as You will. Fill me with Your Holy Spirit." We sat together, hand in hand. Then it happened; such peace as I would never have dreamed possible surged through me, and with it a burst of joy. It was like light, like glory. Suddenly every dark, gloomy shadow in my mind fled and a light like the most radiant morning took the place of those old, dark things, sweeping them out as with a huge broom.

I was elated. I leaped to my feet and began to pace up and down. "It's wonderful!" I declared. "It's wonderful! Praise God! I love Jesus Christ, I love everybody, I love you," and I swept her into a fervent embrace. "Tell you what," I said, "let's go back home. Let's get to work. We're going to have the time of our life all our life!"

I can tell you in complete sincerity that from that moment life was never again the same. Ruth's promise proved a fact. I received an enthusiasm that has never run down. And that peace has remained. The dear Lord has been my Friend all the way. This was the greatest spiritual experience of my life. And it happened on a garden bench in England. A lot of times since then we have journeyed to those glorious English hills and to Lakeland and have sat and prayed and rededicated ourselves on that same bench in that same garden. Jesus Christ has the positive power to change lives. And I ought to know, for He changed my life on that bench long ago.

BACK TO NEW YORK WITH NEW POWER
We returned to New York with a new power, new enthusiasm, revitalized and deepened faith. Exciting things began to happen. I went on radio in a program called "The Art of Living." Over the air as well as in the church we talked about the marvelous things that Jesus Christ can do in human lives when a person surrenders life to Christ. And people listened and responded.

Gradually the church filled up, balconies and all. We had to go to two services, and both were filled to overflowing. Finally, closed circuit television was installed for overflow congregations.

Of course, well do I realize that this new success of the church was not because of any exceptional ability or cleverness on my part to draw in crowds. It was solely due to the fact that the Scripture was being fulfilled. "I, if I be lifted up from the earth, will draw all men unto me."[10] And He always will do just that. It was the drawing power of Jesus Christ which came into action when men and women were persuaded that, through faith in Him and adherence to His word, their lives would take on new meaning. The only way in which I as a person was involved was that, through my complete surrender to Him at Keswick, I became more useful to Him as a channel. And from then until now I witness to anyone, anywhere, at any time about the spiritual, mental, and physical renewal available to any individual through faith in the life-changing and positive power of Jesus Christ.

10. John 12:32

3

Deeper into the Power

ALL THE BOYS AND GIRLS OF MY YOUTH READ and were profoundly conditioned by the Horatio Alger books, classics in the American success literature of that generation. This Horatio Alger tradition motivated me to do the best possible job, to forge ahead, to settle for nothing but big results, to believe that I could succeed.

This motivation spurred me on, kept my nose to the grindstone, made me work and keep on working. About that I had no complaint. I liked to work, always have and still do. I planned, organized, looked ahead. I had goals, and held those goals tenaciously in the conscious mind until, by a process of intellectual osmosis, they seeped into the unconscious. Then I had them, for they had me. Always driven by the urge to do jobs well, I drew upon all my energy, all my initiative; I summoned all the innovative capacity I possessed and came up with ingenious procedures and techniques in the constant struggle to achieve. For what? Just to do the job well, I suppose.

This really describes my pastorate in that early student church, also in Brooklyn, New York, at the Kings Highway Methodist Church. It probably was the reason for the opportunity that came to me next. At the unprecedented age of twenty-eight years I was appointed to the pastorate of one of the most prestigious upstate churches, the University Methodist Church of Syracuse, New York. It was just off the campus of Syracuse University and had previously been pastored, for the most part, by bishops. A major portion of the university faculty attended the church. Here I was, an untried youth from Brooklyn, standing where the ministerial greats had preceded me.

Every day I heard of people who said I was not equal to the job, that I did not have what it takes. Gradually

57

I gloomily shared in this appraisal and was sensitively conscious of my own shortcomings—a carryover of that earlier inferiority feeling. It was imperative that I prove to everyone and to myself especially that I was equal to the opportunity which had come to me. Therefore I relentlessly drove myself, and did achieve some good results if they are to be measured by a full house at church, an excellent program of activity, and a church in satisfactory financial condition. But it was too forced; something was lacking and I was aware of that fact.

I MET HIM ON A TRAIN

But the Lord always provides for our needs. In this case He gave me a deep experience of the power. On a train running between Syracuse and Columbus, I was working on a sermon for the upcoming Sunday that bore the upbeat title, "The Secret of Power." But I was getting nowhere in my preparation; it just would not come. And I knew why; I had no power myself. Finally I put down my pencil and paper and talked to the Lord. I told Him that I knew what my problem was; that my entire attitude was wrong; that my concern was with myself and my own reputation. I admitted to Him that I was striving for success and, to attain it, was depending upon drive, innovation, and the sort of administrative skills anyone would use to make a success of any institution. "We have the worldly achievement, all right," I admitted to the Lord, "but not the life-changing power of Christ."

At this point I learned one of the greatest of all spiritual techniques: that of complete surrender. I found myself saying in my prayer, and meaning it, "Dear Lord, I am fed up with being this way. I do not need to succeed. This is not what I went into the ministry to do. I entered this sacred calling to serve You and lead people to You. So I hereby surrender myself fully. If You want me to fail, that is all right with me. I give myself to You to use wherever and in whatever way You desire. If it is to be a failure, so be it."

I had no sooner offered this simple, sincere prayer than peace such as I had not known up to this point began to steal over me, bringing a wondrous sense of release. Then came an inrushing sense of power and with it a boundless feeling of joy, so much so that I found myself weeping, then laughing. I learned that all-the-way surrender always results in power, joy, and peace. There have been times since when the power seemed to ebb, but always by renewed surrender it would return. So, from personal experience I know whereof I speak in writing about the positive power of Jesus Christ. It is always there for the person who will surrender his life to the Lord and keep on doing so when difficulties arise. The self has to be totally given, and one must be watchful never to fall away.

I returned to my church a different man, with a deeper message and a lot more love for people. I had a new, driving urge to witness for Christ with a more zealous, a more profound persuasiveness. But this new drive never resulted in strain or tiredness. It was drawing upon sources of energy, enthusiasm, and power not previously used by me.

WONDERFUL STORY OF CHARLES K.
This teaching of the power inherent in spiritual surrender, stressed in my book *The Power of Positive Thinking*, brought me many friends, one of whom was Charles K.

He and his wife, Hazel, have been my friends and co-workers for a good many years now. Charles, a businessman in Virginia, had become a full-fledged alcoholic; so much so that he had to have help, and fast, for his life was cracking up.

He made an appointment with the late Dr. William Duncan Silkworth, one of the nation's greatest experts on alcoholism, who worked in a New York City hospital. Receiving Charles into his clinic as a patient, the doctor gave him treatment for some days, then called him into his office. "Charles," he said, "I have done everything that I can do for you. At this moment you are free of your trouble. But there is an area in your brain where you may hold a reservation and that could, in all likelihood, cause you to return to your drinking. I wish that I might reach this place in your consciousness, but alas, I do not have the skill."

"But, doctor," exclaimed Charles, "you are the most skilled physician in this field. When I came to you it was to the greatest. If you cannot heal me, then who can possibly do so?" The doctor hesitated, then said thoughtfully, "There is another Doctor who can complete this healing, but He is very expensive."

"That's all right," cried Charles. "I can get the money. I can pay his fees. I cannot go back home until I am healed. Who is this doctor and where is he?"

"Oh, but this Physician is not at all moderate as to expense," persisted Dr. Silkworth. "He wants everything you've got. He wants you, all of you. Then He gives the healing. His price is your entire self." Then he added slowly and impressively, "His name is Jesus Christ and He keeps office in the New Testament and is available whenever you need Him."

"I need Him now," said Charles softly, "right now. I need Him, and I will give Him myself."

"Great," remarked the doctor. "You will find healing and you will never need to come back to me as a patient; only as a friend. God bless you, and," he concluded, "He will do just that."

Charles walked away from the hospital with a strange feeling that something great was about to happen, or, more accurately, was already happening. It was a dark night, full of rain mixed with snow. Finally, at about eleven o'clock, Charles arrived at our Marble Collegiate Church at the corner of Fifth Avenue and 29th Street. He came there because of having read my books, but we were not acquainted at the time. The spiritual change going on in him had apparently erased time awareness and he found all doors to the church shut and locked at that hour. Only a dim night light filtered muted rays through stained glass windows into the falling snow and rain.

Charles stood for a moment by the door at One West 29th Street. He put his hands on one of the huge marble blocks of which the church is constructed. It made him conscious of strength. He seemed to feel a Presence, a strong Presence in which was wondrous power and love. Reaching for his wallet, he drew out his business card. Taking out his pen, he wrote on the reverse side of the card, "Dear Dr. Jesus, this is Your unworthy servant Charles. Dr. Silkworth says that only You can completely heal me. I hereby now and with all my heart give myself to You. Please touch me in my brain and in my heart with Your healing grace. I love You, dear Jesus." He signed it "Charles" and dropped the card in the mail slot.

HEALING COMES

Charles stood quite still, unconscious of either rain or snow. Suddenly he sensed light and a pervasive warmth spread throughout his entire being, beginning at his head and running down to his feet. It was as if a great big hand touched his head in loving-kindness. He had the same feeling that a person has when after a long illness comes a sense of well-being. He knew for sure that he had been healed. There was no doubt of it at all. He felt clean with a cleanness never before experienced, and with it an awareness of newness. He had been re-born. He was a new man in Christ. Old things long held in his nature were passed away.

We became acquainted through his card dropped in the church mail slot, and I met him later while on a speaking engagement in Virginia. One Sunday I looked down from the pulpit and saw Charles in the congregation. At the moment we were singing the hymn, "What a Friend We Have in Jesus." Just then the sun came out and a long shaft of light passed over the multitude of people, and, for me, it seemed to spotlight Charles. He was singing without a hymnbook. His shoulders were thrown back and a wonderful smile was on his face as he sang, "What a friend we have in Jesus." I looked at him through tears. He indeed knew that Friend, for he had experienced the amazing grace, the positive power of Jesus Christ.

Charles never returned to his old life. He had many problems subsequently, but the power held firm. It never weakened. His healing, which came so dramatically, was permanent. He paid the full price, as the doctor had said he must. He gave himself, all of himself, with nothing held back; and he received the power, the full power, with none of *it* held back. Always as we go deeper into the power we have more power. Such is the marvelous progression of spiritual experience.

ABOUT TO TAKE HER LIFE, THE POWER CAME

This combination of surrender and power is more than equal to any hopelessness, any depth of despair, even to the blackness that can lead to suicide. The positive power of Jesus Christ is infinitely stronger than any negative force arrayed against it, as is evidenced in the return from the brink of suicide described in the following letter:

Dear Dr. Peale,

I gave a testimony in front of a large group of unfamiliar church women who have since become my wonderful new Christian friends who suggested I write you. You and the Lord saved my life three years ago.

I had been a secret alcoholic for thirteen years—secret to everyone but my husband, children and a few friends. Each day at 5:00 P.M. I began to consume as much scotch, bourbon and vodka as I could before Bill got home. I also took Valium, Placydil (for sleep), and Orinase for mild diabetes. At bedtime I drank wine to help me sleep.

My mother was an alcoholic and she had died in a fire in Chicago. Our oldest daughter was hospitalized for adolescent schizophrenia and then became a rebel of the sixties—she was on the pill, marijuana, and LSD. Our other two children suffered from bronchial asthma.

I decided I had the right to drink. During those thirteen years, I was also able to be an executive member of the board of directors of the YMCA, auxiliary president for two years, the co-owner and assistant in my husband's business, a volunteer at a children's hospital, and I developed a volunteer program at our community hospital where I subsequently supervised 214 volunteers daily.

I was getting frightened and lonely without a purpose in my life, living a day-to-day struggle with myself. I was afraid people would find out, afraid to talk on the phone at night, afraid of the hallucinations, afraid of my own physical well-being.

Our girls were married and our son was away at camp. I decided I was ready to take my own life, or live as a recluse, or—? I reasoned that my husband would be much better off with someone else, and certainly another woman would be a better mother.

I made reservations at a motel and put my suitcase in the car. At the last minute, without thinking, I ran back into the house for my Bible and your book, *Power of Positive Thinking*, neither of which I had ever read. I found the motel on the other side of town sitting between two churches. The Seventh-Day Adventist was on one side, and the Baptist on the other. My Room 12 was on the Baptist side!

Instead of going back out to get some food and liquor, I unpacked and started to read your book. I couldn't seem to get enough as I kept reading and alternately reading verses in the Bible that you suggested. I was hungry for more of something I could not possibly conceive of. I kept at it until sometime early morning when I suddenly cried out to the Lord, asking Him to forgive me for all the terrible sins I had committed, and to please, dear God—give me back my life as You want it—and please cure me of alcoholism. In time, I felt His presence in that room. It was heavy, it was powerful, and it was full of love and truth. I had never felt so totally protected in all my life. It was July 7th—a date I will never forget.

I awoke refreshed—and with overwhelming love and awe of Him. I read most of the day until I went into town for some dinner. I was seated at a small table in a restaurant where a complimentary liqueur was served at the end of a meal. At that point I didn't know what to do—I hadn't acquired the habit of refusing a drink, and I reasoned again that this little glass of brandy wouldn't hurt me. As I lifted the glass, there was a compelling motion for me to turn my head to the left. As I turned, I saw the vision of Jesus Christ. He was in translucent shades of purples, reds, golds, and white. His vision stayed there until I paid my bill and left. I wanted to go home.

And all the way home I sang "The Lord's Prayer" and "Onward, Christian Soldiers." When Bill came home and I told him how sorry I was for all the unhappiness and grief I had caused him, he cupped my face in his hands and said, "I've always had faith in you."

It was a little over three years ago that I accepted the Lord into my life. I realized that what I decided to do with my life had to be God's will. I opened my heart to Him. He rewarded me by removing all desire of any alcohol.

I had been so terribly ill—my family had suffered—I had suffered and almost lost—thank God for God! I will always know that somebody cares because God cares. I have a husband who has always had faith in me.

With God, all things are possible, and it is truly wonderful to have a relationship with our Lord. When God is with me, nobody on this earth can be against me. I thank God every night for curing me of alcoholism—and for instilling in me His power of positive thinking in my quest for spiritual growth and well-being.

I also thank Him for you, Dr. Peale. And how can I express my gratitude to another human being except to write you and let you know.

I thank you with such heartfelt gratitude and joy and love.

Sincerely,
Karen F. Kemp

It is a pity that even Christians, regular church-going people, allow themselves to be victims of defeat by the conditions and circumstances of life. Granted that some of these situations may be, or indeed often are, difficult in the extreme, still there is a power that can help any person rise above anything into an area of victory. The mark of a true Christian is, of course, love; but another mark also is joy. It is the joy of overcoming, of victory through the positive power of Jesus Christ working, always working, in the mind and demonstrating itself in the spirit, the undefeatable spirit.

SURGERY NEEDED

I "operated" once on a doctor of medicine, himself a surgeon. Or rather, I should say that upon request I brought the Great Physician, the Supreme Surgeon, into the case.

It happened some years ago in a time of "blatant political corruption," as was charged by metropolitan newspapers in that era. A call came one day saying that a man was seriously ill and asking that I come to see him in the hospital. The name was that of a doctor who was prominent in political circles, and there seemed to be some suspicion of complicity in the manipulation of funds. Why this man should send for me was a mystery until I talked with him in his hospital room.

"I have never met you until now, Dr. Peale," he said, "and I regret to trouble a busy man to come to see me here. But I am in desperate straits. I asked for you because I have heard you preach on several occasions. I know that you believe in the healing power of Jesus Christ, and I wanted to see a minister who is a real believer."

He then went on to explain that as a medical man he naturally tended to diagnose the cause of his own illness, and while obvious physical problems were involved, the root of his sickness, he felt, was not physical or even mental. It was, he said, a spiritual sickness from which he suffered: a pronounced sense of guilt and remorse that gave rise to the physical symptoms which on the surface seemed to be the problem.

He fixed a deeply troubled look upon me and in utmost seriousness, even intensity, said, "I will never get well unless Jesus Christ forgives me and by His mercy heals the lesions, not in my body or even in my mind, but in my soul. For I am sick—sick unto death of a soul sickness. I want you to operate upon me spiritually and in the name of Jesus remove the burden of sin that afflicts my soul and is crushing the life force within me." It was a curious and unforgettable analysis by a man scientifically trained in medicine and surgery, a case which taught me much that would be helpful in my ministry to the ill and troubled in subsequent years.

"All right, doctor," I said, standing by his bed. "I want you to know that I love you in the name of Christ. I am a pastor whose function is the cure of souls. The first step is to clean out or curette the wound. That may be done by a complete catharsis, a flushing out of every evil deed, thought, action, memory. You must let it all flow out. Now start talking, and as you pour it out, I, the servant of the Great Physician, will clear it all away."

Though this was what he knew he needed and indeed wanted, he was a proud man and the process came hard to him. But once he started he sturdily and honestly confessed his wrong thinking and wrongdoing. Finally, quite spent, he looked rather shamefacedly at me and pathetically said, "You must have a low opinion of me."

"Not so," I replied. "I see you as an honest man, a strong man, dealing with your sins after the fashion of a great Christian. For by this act of confession and your desire for forgiveness you now receive God's forgiveness. It only remains for you to forgive yourself. Then you will receive the power. You will be restored to health. Go and sin no more."

As I prepared to leave, the doctor took me by the hand. With a smile he said, "You have a fine bedside manner. You would have been a good doctor." To which I answered, "You remember, do you not, the statement made by a famous physician? 'I treat the patient; God heals him.'" This man lived for a dozen years after this incident and was a dedicated Christian and a healthy person to his life's end. With his keen insight into the devastation of guilt in a human being, he knew that the only curative answer to his health problem was the positive power of Jesus Christ, which indeed made possible his recovery.

NERVOUS BREAKDOWN HEALED

In my ministry I have been drawn into many human situations in which the sense of guilt has been a basic factor in personal misery, even causing sickness, particularly in nervous conditions. I received a letter from a woman in an eastern city who told me that her husband, formerly an active business and civic leader, president of the Rotary Club, past president of the Chamber of Commerce, and involved in other similar activities, was now completely apathetic and lacking in interest in any of his former connections. It seemed that he would sit inert for long periods of time staring straight ahead, seldom speaking, indeed acting totally indifferent to everyone and everything around him. This was so entirely unlike what he had been previously that his wife felt impelled to consult me as well as her physician about her husband's strange behavior, especially in view of the fact that he had been "an enthusiastic exponent, Dr. Peale, of your principles of positive thinking." Whether he had gone overboard on a super-positive attitude and thus depleted his energies by uncontrolled nervous expenditure, or for some other reason had become de-energized, was not clear.

She asked that if I should come to their city on a speaking engagement or other business, would I please let her know and be good enough to see her husband. She assured me that her husband had the very best of medical attention; that, indeed, the doctor himself had hinted his suspicions that a mental, possibly even spiritual, problem might be involved. The physician had volunteered this opinion when she asked if he minded that a pastor be brought in to consult with his patient.

In due course I did have an engagement in that city and notified the lady that I could see her husband in my room in a certain hotel. She telephoned from the lobby at the appointed time to say that her husband was on his way up, and I went to the elevator to meet him. He greeted me with a wan smile and a rather flabby handshake. I noticed as he walked that it was not with a firm stride but rather he seemed to shuffle, hardly lifting his feet from the floor. That, together with the manner in which he held his arms, gave somewhat the impression of a person who had suffered a stroke, but I had been informed that such was not the case. His whole demeanor was that of a man who was a semi-invalid, his natural force much abated.

He sank into a chair with a sigh, but at my urging carried on a reasonably interesting conversation, which at least indicated that his mind was functioning normally. "It's just that the life has been knocked out of me," he explained. "I haven't got any energy, and I must say that I couldn't care less about anything. I guess I'm finished. Washed up. All through. But I did want to meet you, for I have read your books."

"Well," I responded, "they don't seem to have done you much good. They are designed to enhance life, certainly not to contribute to knocking it out of you," I said with a smile.

"Oh, don't get me wrong," he was quick to inject. "Had it not been for your books to hold me up, I'm sure I would now be in my grave."

After a period of establishing a feeling of rapport and understanding, I said, "Jack, have you opened up and talked to anyone about all that stuff you are holding on your chest, or to state it more accurately, in your memory, in your mind?" He looked up, startled.

"What stuff? What do you mean, stuff in my memory, in my mind?"

"Come, now, let's not kid ourselves. You know to what I refer. Your doctor says there is nothing wrong with your physical mechanism, so the inference is that it may be a burden weighing heavily upon your mind, or perhaps even on your soul. This could be the cause of your profound retreat from life, the giving way of your personality force. If this is a proper diagnosis and if you will unload this burden, give it to Jesus Christ. He will clean out your mind, forgive you for anything, everything, and you can be your old self again. In fact, you can be a brand new self, a new creature,[1] as the

1. 2 Corinthians 5:17

70

Bible says. And that is a fact—a great, big, wonderful fact. So, what do you say we get with it and have that marvelous thing happen which is called being born again?"

He looked at me piteously. "How did you know so much about me? Who told you?"

"No one told me and I know no facts about you, but I do know that anyone afflicted as you are, unless he has had a physical accident, must therefore be in deep soul trouble. Now look, I am a pastor, therefore a confidant. I love you and believe in you, and my function is to mediate to you the healing and transforming grace of Jesus Christ who died on the Cross to save sinful men and women."

He started hesitantly to talk, but as the stuff began coming out, his intensity was stepped up until it was obvious that he was finding relief in the exorcism. And what a mass it was, having accumulated over many years—practically every sin in the book, and a lot of sins of desire, though not actually committed in action. When finally he ran down, I asked, "Is that all? Take another look around inside to be sure you have not overlooked anything, for we want to scrape out all this cancerous growth of evil lurking in the soul of a highly respected citizen." He winced a bit at that. "I sure am a heel," he replied, and a few more confessions came forth. Then, "That's all, absolutely all of my lousy history. I can't think of another thing, but that's enough, isn't it? I'm a dirty dog, a skunk, a phony, a no-account. You name it. That's what I am."

"Yes, you are all of that, and so, to one degree or another, are all of us. But you are one more thing that you have not mentioned," I said.

"And what in the world could that be?" he asked.

"A child of God, who is now being redeemed, made over into His likeness.

"Now, Jack," I continued, "let me ask you a question, and I want an honest answer. Are you heartily sorry for your sins?"

"Oh, yes, Dr. Peale. Oh, yes, of course I am, with all my heart."

There was no doubting the sincerity of that response. "O.K., then answer this question. Do you believe that God can and will forgive your sins?"

"Yes, I do, even mine, as bad as they are."

"Ask Him now, aloud, to forgive you." Jack bowed his head, and in a pleading tone that really tugged at my heartstrings he said, "Oh, dear Jesus Christ, my Savior, my dear, loving Friend, please forgive your poor, weak Jack for all the evil things I have ever thought, said, or done, and please take it all away. Please forgive me."

"Now," I said, "thank Him for forgiving you."

"Why, has it already been done?" he asked in surprise.

"It has indeed," I assured him. "Remember the Bible verse, 'What things soever ye desire, when ye pray, believe that ye receive them, and ye shall have them.'[2] Jack, the sincere plea for forgiveness is always granted. Now you must forgive yourself and no longer hold thoughts of your unworthiness. You are free, released, relieved. It is all over, finished. You are a new man in Christ. You have received the positive power of Jesus Christ, your Savior."

2. Mark 11:24

I made a heaping motion with my hands as if to pull together in a heap all that mass of stuff he had emptied out. "No wonder you were ill, with so great a conglomeration of rotten material in your mind and on your soul." I used a motion as if hurling it all away, saying, "As far as the east is from the west, so far hath he removed our transgressions from us,"[3] and "Though your sins be as scarlet, they shall be as white as snow."[4]

Jack sat in deep thought, as did I also. Then he did a strange thing. Slowly getting to his feet, he stretched his arms high above his head. Reaching as far as he could toward the ceiling, he rose up on tiptoe. Then in a strong, exultant voice, almost a shout, he exclaimed, "My, but I feel good!" The relief he expressed was in depth, as if an intolerable weight had been lifted from him, as indeed it had been. As he walked down the hall the shuffling was no more. He moved with a spring in his step and waved a vigorous good-bye as the elevator doors closed.

Jack had a few times of setback, but those were when he indulged in self-condemnation and regret. But when I pointed out that these were intimations of lack of self-forgiveness, he forgave himself over again until gradually the self-forgiveness finally took. These feelings occurred when he tried to make amends for wrongs he had done, as I had told him he must do, but finally when none further could be made, he found peace and full healing. In such manner the positive power of the Great Physician operates in the cure of souls, the healing of persons. The deeper we go into the power, the deeper the power proves to be. There is no limit to the positive power of Jesus Christ.

3. Psalm 103:12   4. Isaiah 1:18

SCHOOL OF PRACTICAL CHRISTIANITY

As I write about the hurts of people and the way many have found healing through Christ, I am impressed anew by the fact that in every church in this land are people who suffer from the same or other kinds of hurts. Look out over any congregation and many of the age-old problems of humanity are represented there. People are indeed hurting, though they may not reveal it.

The mark of a sophisticated person is to dissemble, not to show on that facade called the countenance the hurts that lie in the mind and on the soul. In our ministry we have tried to reach these painful centers in personality and apply Christ's healing and curative balm.

My wife Ruth and I have always worked as a team. It is not *my* ministry but *our* ministry of which I write. She it was who nurtured and developed *Guideposts* magazine into its nearly four-million-subscriber status, now the fourteenth largest magazine in the United States, read monthly by over eleven million people.

Ruth also conceived the idea and led in the development of the Foundation for Christian Living, which sends spiritual literature monthly to nearly one million people throughout the world. She also came up with the idea that we inaugurate what she calls a School of Practical Christianity for pastors. The purpose of the school is not to teach how to have a more successful church, how to preach sermons, how to bring in members, or raise a budget. Rather, the intent is to enrich and refresh ministers spiritually, to make us more aware of the hurts of people, to be truly loving and compassionate, and to learn how to help people more effectively.

Hundreds of pastors have attended these schools,

held at the headquarters of the Foundation for Christian Living at Pawling, New York (65 miles north of New York City), and the attendees have had a new spiritual experience of love and brotherhood. They have gone back to their churches with glowing enthusiasm for Christ and a deep sense of recommitment to the ministry.

Hundreds of letters have been received from ministers and wives who attended the school, one of which is printed here, for it conveys the spirit of in-depth fellowship which exists among Christians when Christ truly is present among them:

> Dear Dr. and Mrs. Peale,
>
> This would have been written before now, but it is difficult to find words to adequately express what I feel in my heart about the marvelous happening we experienced at the 11th School of Practical Christianity. It really was a time where Larry and I were ministered to in many ways, not the least of which we found ourselves feeling we were on a second honeymoon. We've been married 18 years and have 4 children (2 boys—2 girls) and have been through many rough times—so we were ready for it.
>
> Dr. Peale, I'm sure you can't possibly place the names and faces of all of us who were at Pawling for the 11th school, but that's not really important in this letter. Larry and I appreciated the opportunity to be with you and Mrs. Peale the length of time the school offered. We were so impressed that you both would take so much time to be present and share with us much of your life's experiences, which we found very refreshing to hear you relating them to us.
>
> Needless to say, this has been a time of sharing and experiencing that we shall carry through with us for the rest of our lives. I'm now reading your book, Mrs. Peale—*The Adventure of Being a Wife*. There's much of it that hits me right between the eyes, because I find my-

self not measuring up, but I'm confident of the fact that the Lord is working on that and I'm sure will use your book to help me on the road. I'm so glad that I had the privilege to meet you both and see you "in operation," for frankly, there would be some points in your book I probably wouldn't believe or feel were possible, had I not seen how beautifully you both complement each other and work as one organism. God is so beautiful and is much more wonderful than any mere human being could possibly imagine.

Dr. Peale, after one of the meals, Larry and I approached you and I (from my heart) told you "you are even more wonderful than I had imagined." (I didn't mean to embarrass you, for I realized all goodness comes from God.) Then I proceeded to ask, "May I love you?" Well, with the way the term "love" is so mishandled today, there were a few moments of uneasiness (on my part, at least), till I reached over and kissed your cheek. You so graciously revived the atmosphere by commenting that we must be the ones who had a "Cincinnati Reds" sticker on one side of the rear window of our car and "In God I trust" on the other. We were so impressed that you observed something that small (yet not so small, really) in the life of a small-town minister and his wife. It really brought home to me that Jesus really shows through your life, in such a real way, that no one is small in His sight. That is such a rare and beautiful gift to possess, Dr. Peale, and one that is so indispensable in any day and age.

Well, these are just a few things that are on my heart. There's much more, but I'll spare you.

Thanks for such a beautiful time, made possible by you both and others, that will continue to feed us in various moments of our lives. Larry and I will always look forward to that time when our paths shall cross again, whether it be here or in our beautiful future home.

Love,
Peggy Bechtol
(Mrs. Larry O.)

4

Witnessing to the Power

MY OWN CONVICTION ABOUT THE IMPORTANCE of witnessing to one's faith in Christ and demonstrating loyalty to Him in all circumstances has seemingly affected some other Christians with whom I have had contact. Of course, my attitude is probably only one determinative factor in developing their witnessing habits, but some have told me that it did influence them to some extent in becoming more outgoing in testifying to the power.

One who vigorously asserted that my personal policy of witnessing affected his own attitudes was the late Branch Rickey, one-time executive of the St. Louis Cardinals baseball team, then the Dodgers when they were based in Brooklyn, and finally the Pittsburgh Pirates. The owner of the latter is my longtime dear friend, John Galbreath. Some sports authorities have evaluated Branch Rickey as one of the greatest baseball men in the history of the national game. One thing is sure—he was a great and dynamic, always practicing, Christian, one who was never reluctant about witnessing to his faith.

To attend a baseball game with Branch was a rare and unforgettable experience. Seated with him in the Club President's box, I found his conversation was a running combination of baseball, psychology, philosophy, and religion, and it was always exciting and provocative. On one occasion he said to me, "There is a player out there on the field who found Christ a month ago. Yes, sir, he is on the Lord's side now, all right. And," added Branch, always a believer in Christianity as a practical procedure, "his performance has improved, too. And why not? We always do better when we are living the Lord's way." He would pull down those big, beetle-like eyebrows of his and deal you a resounding and painful smack on the knee. "Yes, sir, that guy is in the Kingdom now, and I don't mean maybe."

It did not require much encouragement to get him to tell about this player, for Branch was ever ready with a story, which was always dramatic and fascinating, and told in his own free and easy manner. It seems that the player in question was in a slump and Branch called him in. He loved the boys who played for him, knew their wives and children—even their parents, aunts and uncles in many cases. "What's the matter, son?" he asked. "You seem to be off your game. Aren't you feeling well, or is there something on your mind? Tell old Uncle Branch about it."

"Well, no, Mr. Rickey, I'm just off the beam, but I'll get back on."

"Staying out late nights, I hear, doing some drinking, running around. That's the way I hear it. Especially when the team is on the road." Thus Mr. Rickey, not particularly known for delicacy, laid it on the line, continuing, "Now, son, you've got a sweet wife and nice kids and you ought to be ashamed of yourself. I might as well tell you that you've got to do better, and you will never do better until you start acting better morally."

"But, Mr. Rickey," weakly replied the player, "you know how it is when you are on the road with the boys. You've got to go along—you know the pressures, you know how it is. . . ." His voice trailed off.

"Sure, I know you're a weakling, and I know about the pressures. But where are your inner braces? All you've got to do is be a man. You can be a great man in baseball if you lay off all this stuff—take care of yourself and work hard."

"You're right, Mr. Rickey, I am weak. I just don't have the guts you're talking about."

HE LEADS A BASEBALL PLAYER TO CHRIST

"Want to know how to have guts, how to be strong, how to be a man, son?" asked Rickey. The boy nodded. "It's simple," said Branch. "Get with Jesus Christ. Commit your life to Him. Live His way. Go to church, read the Bible in your family. Pray without ceasing."

"But how do I find Jesus?" asked the young man.

"The only way I know," said Branch Rickey, "is the way I did it. I knelt down and asked Him to come into my life, and He did. It has been many years now, in sunshine and in storm, in good times and bad, and I've had peace and joy in my heart all the way."

"I want the same," quietly said the ballplayer.

"All right," said Rickey, "let's pray, right here, and ask the Lord to take over your life." I asked what happened.

"Well, the boy did as I suggested and I could tell he really meant it, too. And he got the power."

"How do you know that?" I asked.

"One thing was the look on his face. It was beautiful. The guy was absolutely transformed. And since then he has been acting differently. The other players say he is a changed person, and he isn't averse to ascribing his change to Jesus, either."

"How about his playing performance? Did his conversion make any difference in that?"

"Well, all I know is that he is batting close on to .300 and he is on top of that ball every minute. He is O.K.

He will stick. Have no doubt about that. I'm backing him all the way."

Curious, I pointed to the team on the field. "What is his name? Which one is he?"

"Wouldn't you like to know!" Rickey grinned. "Suffice it to say he is one of those nine men you see on that playing field right now."

Admiringly, I told Mr. Rickey that he was a great leader of men, not only in getting the best out of them, but also by putting the best into them. "Well," he said, "I learned it from you, Norman, for you teach that personality really flowers out and capacity is enhanced when Jesus Christ is in charge of a person. You also taught me the importance of witnessing, that it definitely reaches people when you aren't afraid to let them know where you stand, that you are on the Lord's side."

"Oh, you knew and practiced all this long before you started listening to my sermons and reading my books." This he disclaimed by saying that, while he had been reared in a Christian family, he had never consciously witnessed to his faith to any extent nor led people to commit their lives to the Lord until he heard me urging Christians to do so.

"DON'T TALK ABOUT MY FRIEND THAT WAY"
The positive power of Jesus Christ transmitted by creative witnessing was demonstrated by Branch Rickey in still another incident, one that was unique and, to me, unforgettable. It left an indelible impression upon those who were party to it.

Mr. Rickey was in negotiation with some professional football executives for the use of Ebbet's Field in Brooklyn, then the home park of the Dodgers baseball club, which Branch headed. The negotiations were being carried forward daily in a private conference room in the Union League Club on Park Avenue in New York.

Finally, as settlement seemed imminent, Mr. Rickey, to the astonishment of the others, threw down his pencil. "The deal is off," he declared firmly. Completely mystified, the leader of the group expressed his surprise, calling to Mr. Rickey's attention that the negotiations were going along to the satisfaction of both sides so that an agreement seemed in the making. "Now, suddenly you say the deal is off. This is hard to understand, particularly when you stand to make considerable profit."

Rickey glared. "It's because you, sir, are constantly speaking of a Friend of mine. This Friend means everything to me and I'm not going to sit here and listen to my Friend's name being used as you are doing. I repeat, the deal is off. It isn't that important to me to make some money." It seems that the man's conversation was profane in nature and he was constantly saying, "Jesus Christ" this and "Jesus Christ" that. He looked at Mr. Rickey and said, "I get you. I am very sorry. He is a Friend of mine, too. I should not so use the Holy Name. You will not hear me do that again. Thank you for calling my attention to what has become a habit—a bad habit."

Rickey relented and the negotiations continued for several days. During one session Mr. Rickey suddenly suffered a seizure which was thought to be a heart attack, though it subsequently did not turn out to be that. However, he was at once put to bed in the club and I was sent for. Mrs. Rickey was by his side. He seemed somewhat exhausted but mentally alert. "Say a prayer for Branch," Mrs. Rickey asked, and I did so with much feeling, for I loved this man.

When I had finished, Branch grinned. "That was a pretty good prayer," he said. "Now let me pray." Whereupon he talked to the Lord in the most beautiful, loving fashion, albeit with characteristic ruggedness. It was most affecting, and we were deeply moved. Then I noticed a man standing in a far corner of the bedroom whom I had not noticed previously. It was the leader of the negotiations team, the man who had profanely used the name of Christ. He moved toward the door and into the hall, motioning me to follow. Tears were on his face; his voice choked up. "That man," he said feelingly, indicating the bedroom, "is the greatest human being I ever knew. He is what you call a man." Branch Rickey survived that crisis and lived for some years thereafter.

In these incidents, connected with the life of a great sports leader, a powerful business executive, and a dedicated Christian, there is a notable example of the positive power of Jesus Christ in action. If more Christians were excited enough about their faith to witness in similar manner and thus lead people to Christ, this generation could bring about one of the greatest spiritual eras in history, with resulting benefit to all mankind. Businessmen and women are taking the lead in this area and many are losing their one-time reticence in making known their Christian commitment. There is a speaking circuit in this country made up of national business conventions, trade association annual meetings, regional sales rallies, Chambers of Commerce, and motivational meetings. I have been speaking on this circuit for over forty years. Lately I have been impressed by the fact that more and more people at these gatherings are enthusiastically and very naturally bearing testimony to their faith. The same thing is happening in one-to-one encounters.

Most of the speakers with whom I share the platform invariably include a spiritual note or message in their talks. These have included such well-known speakers as Art Linkletter, Paul Harvey, Zig Ziglar, Ira Hayes, Cavett Robert, and others. Recently, on a speaking tour at huge sales rallies in the major cities of Australia, I was impressed by the Christian witness, both on and off the platform, of Mr. Ziglar, who has published two books, *See You at the Top* and *Confessions of a Happy Christian*, both of which feature his own personal story of conversion.

In Australia, at dinner following a meeting addressed by Mr. Ziglar and myself, one of the most successful automobile salesmen of the country said, "You Americans always bring in a spiritual note at these general public sales meetings. Our people never do that. It rather startled me, I must admit, but I like it. Still, I wonder why you Americans always include a Christian witness."

"Well," I answered, "at a sales gathering, speaking on a motivational theme, our object is to stimulate self-improvement. And we do not believe real self-improvement is possible apart from God working in our lives."

"That is a good reason," he said. "I believe that the basic potential put in us by the Creator requires God's help to bring it out and into action. But we never think to talk about that in a business meeting."

"YOU ARE A CHRISTIAN, AREN'T YOU?"
There is, of course, the power of silent witnessing, the impressive effect of genuinely living the Christlike life.

Always, actions speak louder than words. "By this all men will know that you are my disciples, if you have love for one another."[1] I shall long remember the self-centered, petulant, and ultra-favored girl who came to New York City from a small West Virginia town and got caught up in the so-called "new morality" of the Big Apple. For her it turned out to be a rotten apple and she came to Marble Collegiate Church broken and desperate, looking for help.

We introduced her to our Young Adult group, where she found a large number of young people, many of whom had been through similar experiences but who in our church had found new and satisfying answers built around Christ as the center. They had rebuilt their lives on a substantial and spiritual basis, and this young woman was astonished to find such happy, released, and well-organized individuals. She couldn't believe such persons existed in New York City, people who had found a new and exciting life style and around no less than Jesus Christ, whom she had known as a youngster but had bypassed as a young adult.

Her personal problem was a temperament that, to say the least, was volatile. Totally lacking in patience and urbanity, she had developed a personality that rubbed people the wrong way and a temper that often flared forth in anger. She was received into this Christian group even though it became apparent that she was a difficult person due to her tensed-up disposition. Irritation and caustic reaction flashed out of her at the slightest provocation.

She was brought into contact with our Institutes of Religion and Health and persuaded to have counseling,

1. John 13:35, RSV

where our highly trained counselors sought to get at the roots of her hateful personality characteristics. But to no avail. Then one night in a small group session another girl, a beautiful, sophisticated-appearing person, told of her own experience with an "inflamed and ultra-sensitive nature" and how she had surrendered her whole self to Christ and had been miraculously changed so that she was inwardly and outwardly peaceful, quiet, and controlled. The girl from West Virginia was profoundly impressed, for it seemed that her own case was precisely described by this other person's experience. She spoke frankly of her problem in that group session and, surrounded as she was by dedicated Christians, she was led to completely commit her life to Christ's control. The positive power of Jesus Christ proceeded to effect a remarkable change in her life and in her attitudes. The amazing grace deeply penetrated her nature.

She was a student nurse in a New York City hospital. One day she had a particularly cantankerous and unreasonable patient assigned to her, an old lady who was excessively demanding and extremely difficult. Our West Virginia girl, who had previously been "driven up the wall by this old goat," was now quiet, loving, and patient. She took the old lady in stride, was kind and considerate.

One night, after the patient has been particularly difficult, the nurse was smoothing down the coverlet of the irascible patient's bed when the woman looked up and said, "You are a Christian, aren't you?"

"Yes," said the girl, "I am. I have committed my life to Christ. But why do you ask?"

"Because," said the old lady with the sweetest smile she had ever shown, "otherwise you could not have been so patient and kind with an old she-devil like me.

I like you, young lady." From then on the patient was much more tractable and soon she got well. She left the hospital, but never a Christmas went by that our young lady did not receive a card, "To one of the sweetest Christians I ever knew." Here again the positive power of Jesus Christ revealed itself in a life-changing situation in which the witness of new life touched others with creative effect.

IN A BROOKLYN BAR

The boy was halfway drunk, all-the-way discouraged, and broke except for one lonely nickel in his pocket. He was sitting at the end of a bar in Brooklyn looking without enthusiasm at his reflection in the long mirror. The radio near him was blaring out the evening news. Suddenly the newscast ended and a voice announced that a preacher was scheduled next who would talk on the subject, "You can live an exciting life." "Nuts," said the boy to no one in particular. "Life is a flop, a washout. What do you mean, 'You can live an exciting life'?"

But he had nothing else to do. What could anyone do with only a nickel in his pocket? So he listened to the preacher as he told how to live an exciting life. And according to the boy the talk made sense. He felt strangely moved, even excited, as if his own destiny was at stake. He even felt that a new life was in store for him. Then the preacher said, "Wherever you are, come on over to our Marble Collegiate Church at the corner of Fifth Avenue and 29th Street. We will have a meeting going until about 10 P.M. Come on over. We want to help get you started on a wonderful and exciting life."

The boy fingered the nickel. It was all he had. If he

spent that he would have nothing. His pocket would be absolutely empty. A nickel wasn't much, but when it was all you had it was something. This was back when you could travel anywhere on the New York subway system for five cents, the fare that every mayoral candidate for years pledged himself to preserve.

The boy, moved by a power beyond himself, slid off the bar stool, walked to the corner, put his nickel in the subway turnstile, and took a train to 29th Street, Manhattan. He arrived at the church and was welcomed by the Young Adult people and soon found himself eating some delicious refreshments. Then he found himself in a small group where all the participants were enthusiastically talking of how much Jesus Christ had helped them, how He had changed their lives from failure, poverty, and defeat. The boy soon realized he was where he wanted to be. These people were just like him—same problems, same failures. The only difference was that they had found the answer; he had not.

The witnessing in the meeting got to him. If the lives of these young people could be changed as they had been, why couldn't the same thing happen to him? One of the group drove him home to Brooklyn. The next week he got a job. He had been looking for one, but had drifted down to that nickel. Every Sunday night thereafter he went back to the church, and one night he entered into a wonderful, meaningful spiritual experience. He gave his life to the Lord in a genuine act of surrender to the will of God. He had grown spiritually over the weeks and was ready both mentally and spiritually for a new life style, one totally different. It was as exciting as the minister had promised in that radio talk he had listened to in the Brooklyn bar.

Later he found a girl in the church group and presently they were married. He was so overwhelmed by all that God had done for him that he just had to tell the story to as many others as would listen. He went to college, to a seminary, and became a minister. He is still telling the message everywhere of the positive power of Jesus Christ. He ought to know, for did not the power reach him as he sat, glum and discouraged, in a Brooklyn bar with a lonely nickel in his pocket? His life became an impressive witness to that power.

SHOULD HE KILL HIMSELF?

There seemed no hope at all. Everything had gone badly—indeed, so badly that the only way out appeared to be to end it all with a pistol shot to the head. The pistol lay in the desk drawer in the hotel room. It was loaded and ready. All it took was the nerve to pull the trigger. When that was done, all his troubles would be over. Or would they? Who knew?

Deep, dark depression had settled down on the mind of this young businessman. His affairs were in an indescribable mess. In addition, his personal life had deteriorated into chaos. All of his hopes and expectations had crashed about him; he was pressed for payment of debts which he could not meet. His whole existence seemed to be a shambles. Perhaps in his dark thoughts he was no longer capable of rational thinking, and possibly things were not as bad as they seemed. But to the person immersed in gloom, what seems to be is as formidable as if the actuality existed.

This man, Bob, had walked the streets in a desperate state of mind. Finally returning to his meager hotel room, he had thrown himself upon the bed, only to stare at the ceiling. Then he sat for long periods, head in hands, thinking—but not thinking, the mind twisting around in never-ending circles that came out at no end.

A hotel night clerk, member of our Marble Collegiate Church, became concerned by this guest's obvious discouragement and talked with him as he had opportunity. Being sensitive to human need, he picked up the thought, "a potential suicide," though it had not been specifically mentioned. The night clerk telephoned the church and Harold, one of our members, a man of great capacity for helpfulness and with a loving understanding of people in trouble, went to the hotel. The clerk introduced him to Bob with the remark that Harold, a successful businessman, might have some helpful suggestions for straightening out his affairs.

The two men sat for several hours in the coffee shop, Harold skillfully feeling his way into the dark and agitated mind of the man sitting across the table. He got Bob to talking, and his troubles and despair gushed out in a tumultuous stream of words that flowed on as the clock pushed two in the morning.

Then Harold began to talk about his own experiences in business and in life, and now and then the name of Jesus would appear, always in a perfectly natural and unstrained manner, just enough to convey a new thought to the troubled man. "Well," said Harold, looking at the clock, "guess we'll have to knock it off, old boy. Time we both hit the hay. Tell you what—kneel by your bed and say a little prayer like you did when you were a kid. Bet you it'll make you sleep better. And I'll pray for you when I get ready for bed. I'll see you tomorrow for lunch, O.K.?" It was O.K. with Bob, who said, "Thanks, Harold. You're a great guy. You've helped me a lot."

THE POSITIVE POWER GOES TO WORK

Harold's subtle witnessing paid off, for when the two met for lunch the next day Bob looked more refreshed and rested. "I felt so peaceful after unloading my troubles that I actually had a full eight hours' sleep. And," he added a bit hesitantly, "I did as you said. It was the first time I had prayed in years, I'm ashamed to admit, and it wasn't much of a prayer at that."

"What did you say in your prayer?" Harold asked. "That is, if you don't mind telling me."

"I didn't exactly know what to say," Bob replied, "so I just said, 'Dear Jesus, I love You. Please help me. And then I will help You. Amen.'"

"That was a great prayer," said Harold. "It was all there—you love Him—He will help you—then you will serve Him. That is prayer that's real. You are on your way to a better life." And over the weeks that followed, Harold and his wife, Mary, with other young people in the spiritual sharing group of modern New York City, led Bob step by step out of the darkness and into the light. One day at lunch Bob handed Harold a pistol. "Get rid of it for me, please," he said.

Over the years I remember Bob as one of the happiest men I have ever known, a great, sturdy, victorious Christian who blessed the life of everyone who met him. The positive power of Jesus Christ had done yet another tremendous work in a human being.

MEANWHILE A GIRL

Hazel was her name and she was anything but happy. Though she had a good job in business, her life was empty and hollow. She felt that surely there was something that could give satisfaction and peace and joy, but it was altogether lacking. Meaningful life constantly eluded her. Perhaps going to church might help, she decided, and she started attending services at our Marble Collegiate Church. To her surprise, she found it a happy place. There actually was laughter in church and the people sitting around her seemed to have a glow on their faces.

The church was packed every Sunday, and the atmosphere seemed to be full of excitement and expectation, as if everyone knew that something wonderful was going to happen. Later Hazel was to meet Mary Brinig, one of the most dynamic Christians we ever had in our church, and in her own attractive and persuasive manner Mary shared her own faith with the girl.

Anyway, this young woman was now getting involved in that spiritual climate of the church and her personality began to open to it as a rose opens to the sun. Then she was invited into a group of New York City young business people who had themselves been seeking something vital and were finding it in depth. As a result they were becoming truly Christ-centered, and a whole new, exciting and joyous life was opening up for them.

Hazel found it, too. So deep was her experience of Christ living within her that she became completely changed in her entire nature. The uncertainty, the emptiness, the hunger for something better passed away, for she had found that something better. She was full to overflowing. Her deep hunger was satisfied.

Hazel became so positively radiant that the difference in her at the office was marked. "What's happened to Hazel?" her associates asked one another. "Oh, I know," said one, "she's in love. Only being in love can make anyone look that way." Finally Hazel was asked, "What has changed you so? Are you in love?" Hazel's eyes shone with glorious light and a beautiful smile was on her face. "Yes, I am in love. I've met Jesus. I'm in love with Him," she said softly.

Then one day at church Bob saw Hazel and was impressed by the radiance of her countenance, the light in her eyes, the happy effervescence of her personality. He fell in love with her forthwith. She found the same depth of victory and joy in him. Came a day at the altar of the church when I united these two in marriage. It was a wonderful marriage that grew in happiness. These two changed people were witnesses to a power, a wonder-working power; the positive power of Jesus Christ.

My pastoral activities are not restricted to my own church, for I am on the road so much of the time that many of my most telling opportunities for witnessing to the power occur in airports, on airplanes, in auditoriums in connection with speeches, in restaurants, hotel lobbies, indeed just about anywhere and everywhere.

For example, I recall the sophisticated woman who approached me in the Pittsburgh airport. She was, I guessed, rather on the rough side, and her language supported that quick appraisal. "Say, Reverend," she began, "I've got a question that really has me bothered. I'm going to put it to you straight and I want a straight answer—no ifs, no buts, just the facts."

"O.K.," I responded, "give it to me straight and I'll give it back to you straight. Let's have it."

"What I want to know is, if I knock myself off will I go to hell?"

"If your life has been lived so as to make hell the appropriate place for you, that is where you will end up. But if you've got the guts to live and to change, to have faith in Christ and to find God, you will go to heaven."

She blinked. "Boy, that is laying it on the line. You don't pull any punches, do you?"

"Not with you, I don't, for I read you as a strong personality. While you may have messed up your life, you have the basic strength of character to reverse yourself and become an equally good and happy individual. As a matter of fact, I rather like you for your forthrightness. You've got something real in you."

"And I like you, too, for you're the first person since my sainted mother died who ever said they believed in me. Thanks for that." And I thought I noticed the suggestion of tears in her eyes.

Her airplane was about ready for departure, and mine was also. There was no time for further talk, but I asked, "Got a Bible at home?"

"Yes, one is somewhere around. Mother gave it to me when I joined the church as a child."

"Tell you what; I suggest you read the Gospel of John and also Matthew, Mark, and Luke. Then come home to Jesus, to the life your mother tried to point out to you. Do that and you will find peace and joy and the power to live. You will have no further thoughts of 'knocking yourself off.'"

She took me by the hand. "Thank God He sent you to this airport today," and she rushed away to her plane. A few weeks later a card was in my mail signed only, "The woman from Pittsburgh airport," and the brief message was, "I found the Lord. Praise His name. All is O.K. now. Thanks and God bless you."

One never knows what a witness will accomplish or what it can mean to a person in distress. Always it can be related to the positive power of Jesus Christ, of that there can be no doubt.

5

Some Amazing Results of the Power

BY CONSTANTLY STRESSING THE MESSAGE THAT faith in Jesus Christ changes lives, and by witnessing to this phenomenon in every possible medium—pulpit, books, speeches, and one-to-one relationships—I have over the years seen some amazing results of the power.

One man who experienced this power some years ago was Bill Moyer. Bill was a prominent businessman in New York City, controller of the Penn Road Corporation with offices in a hotel owned by that corporation. I did not know Mr. Moyer at the time. He came to my attention because he responded to the invitation to accept Christ given at a church service. This was couched in words that promised a better and more satisfying life to anyone who desired it.

One Sunday evening, impelled by a strange restlessness, Mr. Moyer went for a walk. For a long time, despite his notable business success, he had been plagued by a feeling of emptiness and dissatisfaction. He was a man of integrity and high moral character, a good-living man, but he felt no joy, no sense of meaning, no assurance that his life counted for anything, really. He had made it big, but when he arrived the feeling was, "Well, so what? What's it all about or really worth?"

So on this particular Sunday evening he left the hotel where he lived and headed toward Fifth Avenue with no definite destination in mind, thinking vaguely that he might walk to Washington Square and back. Turning south on Fifth Avenue, on the west side of the street, he proceeded from Thirty-second Street downtown. The time was seven forty-five and he saw large crowds pouring into our church at the northwest corner of Fifth Avenue and Twenty-ninth Street. He was astonished. He had no idea that people went to church in such obvious numbers. He glanced at the bulletin board outside which announced the title of the sermon, "Joy and Power for You." That, plus curiosity, prompted him and, thinking how strange that he should do so, he joined the crowds and secured one of the last few seats in the rear balcony. Destiny walked with him.

He was charmed by the beauty of the church and the lovely music. He found himself strangely moved by the old hymns which brought back memories. But what really got to him was the obvious happiness of the people seated around him. They seemed to enter into the service in no formal or perfunctory manner but with actual enthusiasm. The atmosphere of the church seemed pervaded by a quality of spirit he could not recall ever having felt in church. Actually, he had not been in church for twenty years, but the spirit was so definite that he began to respond with deep feeling.

The sermon, to which he listened intently, was a simple, persuasive talk based on the fact that a person can live a life of peace, joy, and victory by relating himself in an all-out manner to Jesus Christ as Savior. The talk was interspersed with stories about people who had found such new life. The joyousness of spiritual experience came through in spontaneous humor that rocked the great congregation with laughter, even as the next moment moved everyone to tears. It was, he thought, all so natural, so beautiful, and really quite wonderful. He began to reach mentally for what he was seeing, hearing, and feeling.

At the conclusion of the sermon I called attention to a card in the pews which one could use to register the decision to commit oneself to Christ. There was a place for name and address. Mr. Moyer reached for a card, studied it, then put it in his pocket. He left the church deeply moved by the feeling that perhaps at last he was on the way to finding what he so much wanted, what his inner nature was deeply reaching for.

MIRACLE AT THE MAIL CHUTE

Monday morning my secretary notified me on the office intercom that "a man named William Moyer says it's very urgent that he speak with you." When he came on the wire he said, "Did you receive my decision card signed last night?"

"No," I replied. "Perhaps it will come in a later mail."

"Well," he continued, "I just cannot wait for that. I know you must be very busy, but this matter is so important that I must ask you to come to see me at once. It's only a few blocks." Somehow the intensity of his feeling came through and I immediately dropped everything and proceeded to his office. I was led past numerous secretaries to the very plush setting of the chief financial officer of this large corporation. There I met Bill Moyer, a quiet man of impressive bearing and obvious great ability.

"Here's my story," he said, getting right down to the business that had brought us together. He told of his personal feelings, of the walk of the previous evening, and of attending the church service. Then he said, "I came back to the hotel and turned in early. As I emptied my pockets I laid that card from the pew on my writing table, all the time thinking of what it meant.

"I went to bed and at once to sleep. But at two A.M. I awakened. I recall exactly, for I looked at the clock. And, sir . . . " He hesitated a long time. He was by nature a restrained person who did not reveal emotion. Then he continued, "To my astonishment I was weeping, and that was strange for I felt very happy. Besides,

I'm not a weepy kind of person. I couldn't figure what could possibly have come over me. Once I wondered if I was going to die. But I knew that could not be. I felt too good for that. Sitting down at the table, I saw the card from the church. Then I knew. Jesus Christ was touching me. He really was." Moyer turned to me a face filled with faith mixed with a sort of wonderment.

Continuing, he said, "I signed the card surrendering myself to Christ, put on my bathrobe and went down the hall to the mail chute. I dropped the card into the slot and watched it flash by on its way down. And I've got to tell you that something incredible happened to me right then and there, that very minute. It was as though a big, kindly hand rested on my head. Every old, unhappy thing that had ever accumulated in my mind was swept out, and such a feeling of peace and joy as I'd never known came over me. It was . . . it was as if Jesus Himself took me to Himself."

Then to my surprise Bill started to sob, and he was obviously mortified at so doing. It's a bit painful to watch a strong, dignified man cry, but I sat silent, though myself deeply moved. "Forgive me," he said presently. "I had no idea I could be that emotional, but what has happened to me is so very wonderful."

"It truly is wonderful, Bill," I agreed, "for you are having one of the most beautiful spiritual experiences I've ever seen any person have. The reason for the emotion is that the Lord, who has called you, is reaching into the deep places of your inner life, of your soul, into the great area where you are to find peace and joy for the rest of your days." From that moment I loved this man and honored him as one of the greatest, humblest, most dedicated Christians I have ever known. By the miracle at the mail chute, the old life fell away and a marvelous new life came into being.

From that morning onward Bill Moyer could not do enough for the Lord and the church. Mrs. Peale had been praying for a certain sum of money to finance a missionary project. Without any conversation or previous information on the subject, Mr. Moyer sent a check to me which, strangely enough, was for the exact amount needed. "The Lord told me you need this for something you have in mind," he explained in a note accompanying the check.

One day at lunch he said, "Norman, you need a chauffeur to drive you and Ruth around doing all the good you do. I'm employing one for you."

"Oh, no thanks, Bill," I said. "That's just like you, but I'm a country boy at heart. I'd feel foolish with a chauffeur. Give that money for something else sometime." At still another lunch in the big dining room of the hotel an organist was playing. "That's a nice organ," I commented.

"Do you want it?" he asked. Surprised, but as a matter of fact not so surprised, for I was getting used to Bill's quick decisions, I said, "Sure. We could use it in one of our prayer chapels."

"O.K., I'll send it over." He did just that, with the rather lame excuse that some men had complained that this organ music interfered with their talking business at the noon hour. In every way this new and vital disciple of Jesus served the Lord, so great was his gratitude and joy.

A few years later Bill died. The Lord must have loved him so much that He wanted Bill Moyer nearer to Him. I took him on a special train to Philadelphia for burial.

The train was filled with business leaders from all over the eastern part of the United States, going to the last resting place with this beloved and admired man. One after another they came to me saying, "What did you do to Bill? What a change in a man!"

"I did nothing," I protested, "nothing at all. Someone else did."

"We know," they would say softly; "we know." And as one of his associates said, "Bill's experience was a great demonstration of the power of the Lord to change a good man into a wonderful man." When Bill's will was probated he had designated a large provision to "carry on the work of the dear Lord Jesus." And when, later, his sister died, she, too, left a sizeable bequest to the church, saying, "In gratitude to our Lord for what He did for my beloved brother." I shall ever revere the memory of this man and his sister, for in this experience was demonstrated once again the amazing results of the power.

UNHAPPY FACE IN THE CROWD

These same amazing results continue to occur, with similar power and far-reaching consequences, in the lives of the now, the modern, the with-it people. It is clearly evident that Jesus Christ continues to put His miraculous touch upon human beings today; indeed, it increasingly appears that the Lord is more sought after and more accepted currently than at any time in years.

There are two congregations at Marble Collegiate Church—one composed of members who live in all sections of the New York area, the other made up of persons from out of town who come from everywhere in this country and abroad. These latter are variously tourists visiting the city, men and women in town on business, buyers in for the market. Almost always over weekends hotels are filled with people staying over for one purpose or another and a surprisingly large number attend our services. They queue up outside the church on Fifth Avenue in lines often reaching around the block on Thirtieth Street as far as Broadway. Most of these visitors I never have the pleasure of meeting personally, but some I do come to know. For not a few out-of-town business people visit the church so regularly that they come to feel the church is a spiritual home for them, and we in turn think of them as associate members.

One face in the crowd caught my attention. This man, whom I did not know, began to appear regularly in the congregation. I was particularly drawn to him because of the darkness and gloom written on his face. This stood out because of the contrast from the regular run of worshipers, who seemed to have happy and peaceful faces. But this man's face was stamped with unmistakable and intense unhappiness, poignantly so.

After one service it was necessary for me to leave immediately to fill another speaking engagement, and in hurrying to my car I encountered this man on the sidewalk by the church. Shaking hands, I bade him welcome and stated that I had noticed him several times in the congregation. He explained that he came to the city quite regularly on business and always stayed over for our Sunday morning service even though he might have returned to his home on Saturday. About to enter my car, for some reason I said, "I'm sorry that you are so unhappy. You are too fine a fellow to be that way. If you ever feel that I can be of any help, let me know." He looked startled, fumbled for words, then quickly walked off. Pulling away from the curb, I wondered if I had hurt or misjudged my man. But there was also the definite feeling of being guided in what I had said to him.

A couple of weeks later a letter came from this man marked "Personal and Confidential." Referring to my remark, he said I had correctly read him, that he was indeed in great trouble. It was, he asserted, getting too much for him to carry and he requested an appointment. I wrote him, suggesting a date and time, and he arrived at my office punctually.

"The matter I have to talk with you about is most painful and difficult for me," he began, "and is this interview in strict confidence?"

"Of course," I replied. "I am a pastor, and as such receive every communication in confidence and sacredly keep it so. Furthermore, you may be assured that whatever you may reveal will not reduce my respect and regard for you as a person. Indeed, the more honest an individual is in cleansing himself, the more a pastor's respect for him increases."

He rather winced at the latter remark. "You must be able to see into a person," he commented. "First, you read my unhappiness. Now you see the evil in me. Well, you are right, for I am a thief, a downright dirty, double-crossing crook. At home I'm considered an upright, moral Christian man, but they don't know what I really am—a low-down skunk, a common thief. I guess that is the unhappiness you saw, for I am miserably unhappy. I'm full of guilt, and scared to death that I will be found out and thrown into prison, my family disgraced forever."

"You are an O.K. guy," I said, "not one of those phonies who occasionally come to me when in trouble and blame everyone else for the wrong they do. You are a man, a real man. You stand right up to it, take the blame fully on yourself, call yourself a skunk and a dirty, low-down, double-crossing thief with no evasion, no rationalization—straight-shooting and forthright. I like you. You are a man Jesus Christ can do something with—a man-sized sinner. You are a sinner and you know it. I like you, and so does the Lord like you. What have you done? Stolen money, or somebody's wife, or both—or what?"

THIEF COMES CLEAN

The story was that this man (I'll call him Ernest, though that was not his name) was helped through college by a kindhearted man who operated the biggest enterprise in his town, and after graduation brought Ernest into his office as bookkeeper. Gradually, as the business greatly expanded, he advanced to the position of controller. His boss's trust in him was implicit and in time Ernest came to handle all monetary affairs pretty much on his own. Apparently his financial sense was acute and skilled; therefore, he was extremely important to the company.

Then Ernest began to "play" the stock market and his financial insights were not so sharp in this area, with the result that he incurred some heavy losses. Some of the company's liquid funds were handy. He could try the market again and, with better luck, recover the losses and return the money. This thought he repulsed. Indeed, he was shocked that it had even come to mind. But it came again, and then again, until the thought resulted in action. Always the thought is the ancestor of the deed. He then began to make some money on that which he had "borrowed."

"How much have you taken your employer for, now?" I asked. "And skip the other details." He shoved a slip forward. On it were figures; $171,434. "Is this what you took, or does it represent in part money you made on the stolen money?"

"When that is added in, I owe him $218,560."

"Well, to say the least, you are an accurate accountant. Does he suspect you?"

"No, not at all. The business is in good shape; plenty of capital assets, adequate cash flow."

"How much do you think you owe your boss?" I asked.

"I owe him what I took plus what I made, for I made it with his money and rightfully it all belongs to him."

"All right, now another question: Could you put this total of $218,560 back into the business without the boss ever being aware of what you did?"

"Oh, yes, but wouldn't that be compounding the dishonesty?" he asked.

"Your moral sense is keen," I said. "The only thing, then, that remains is to confess the whole affair to him. Can you raise the money to pay back this theft?"

"Yes, but I will have to mortgage everything I have and that will leave me about strapped."

"But with peace of mind," I suggested.

He nodded. "That's for sure."

"What shall I do?" he then asked. "I need guidance."

"O.K., let's go where guidance comes from." We both prayed, then had a period of silent prayer. "What guidance do you get?" I asked.

"That I go to my boss, level with him, pay him back

the money, resign my job, and be prepared to take what's coming to me."

I nodded. "That checks with me."

"He is a kindly man, but he has no use for dishonesty. I'll be looking for a job, and nowadays that's not so easy."

"Well," I said, "you know what the Bible says."

"I sure do," he replied. "'The way of transgressors is hard.'"[1]

"Right; this soft generation needs to be taught that tough truth."

But I felt it necessary to tell him that we were not finished with him yet; that he had to be sorry, really sorry, not that he was in trouble, but that he had sinned; and that he must ask God not to get him out of trouble but to get the sin out of him. He asked this mercy from God with a most impressive sense of contrition. "Cleanse my soul of all sin, regardless of what happens to me," he asked humbly.

On his next trip to New York I saw Ernest in the congregation but hardly knew him. His facial expression was one of happiness and peace. The glumness was erased. Later he said to me, "I went to my boss and blurted the whole story out, even telling him I had told you all about it. He sat very still looking out the window for a long while. Then do you know what he said? 'Ernest, you must have been living in hell for a long time, a good man like you doing wrong. I feel so sorry for you.' He was thinking of me, not of what I stole from him. What do you know about that!"

"He must be a great human being," I said. "Then what happened?"

1. Proverbs 13:15

"I gave him the check. 'Where did you get this big amount?' he asked.

"'I mortgaged everything, sir, and added all my savings.' He took the check, saying, 'Taking up your belt will be good for your soul, Ernest.'"

"Wise man," I commented.

"Then, what do you think?" Ernest asked.

"Can't guess," I responded.

"He said, 'Ernest, tomorrow morning report to the sales manager. I'm putting you in sales on commission plus a small drawing account for expenses. Then, son, you just take your life and put it in the hands of the Lord Jesus Christ and ask Him to make a good, honest salesman of you. And Ernest,' as he stood up to dismiss me, 'remember what Jesus said to the woman taken in adultery?'

"'What, sir?' I asked.

"'"Go, and sin no more."'"[2]

"Smart boss," I commented admiringly. "Do just that. Trust Jesus to help you, and you will come out O.K." Which indeed he did. Gone thereafter was that one unhappy face in the crowd; a happy face took its place. The positive power of Jesus Christ produced yet another amazing result in a man's life. As a footnote, Ernest turned out to be just as good a salesman as he had been a controller, which says something about that wise Christian employer's keen insights.

OUT WITH ANOTHER WOMAN

One of the chief signs of rot in our society is the deterioration of marriage. Cicero said, "The empire is at the

2. John 8:11

fireside." That is to say, the strength of the nation is in the home. And of course marriage is the foundation stone of the home. As the Bible says, "Except the Lord build the house, they labor in vain that build it."[3] So, ultimately, Christ is the cornerstone of marriage and marriage is the foundation of the home and the home is the basis of the state. Therefore, Christ and His power to save are vital in still another area of human experience; namely marriage, the home and family, and, ultimately, the nation itself.

How the positive power of Jesus Christ works in marital situations is illustrated by the story of the woman who telephoned me one night from a western city. She was sobbing. Finally I distinguished some words hysterically spoken. "I've just found that my husband is out with another woman." She then proceeded to go into a tirade, punctuated by sobs, in which she revealed surprise, shock, complete brokenheartedness. "Oh, what shall I do? What shall I do?" she cried.

"Well," I said, "the first thing is to stop crying and stop talking. You apparently telephoned me thinking I could help you, and I think I can; but you will have to quiet yourself. To handle this situation we must think— coolly, factually, objectively. And that cannot be done under heated-up emotion. So, first thing, let's cool it; quiet down. Let's practice rational thought about the matter."

"Oh, I know, but I would never have believed it. I just know I've lost him. I'm hopeless."

"Being hopeless isn't going to get you anywhere. Besides, it is being plain stupid to get hopeless, as you are saying. That is giving up before you start. Now listen,

3. Psalm 127:1

I want you to repeat after me the following; listen carefully and give this back to me: "Hope thou in God: for I shall yet praise him." In a weak voice she repeated those words from the 42nd Psalm, the fifth verse. "Oh, come on," I told her, "louder and with real force. Those words mean you are putting your hope in God and that the day will come when you will praise Him for the wonderful things that will happen. Now say the words again," which she did, this time with considerably more conviction. "Now, let's do some thinking," I said. "Tell me the story in sequence, calmly, and no more crying."

She went on to say that she telephoned me when she learned about her husband because she didn't know where else to turn. She and her husband had long been readers of my books. When she experienced the shock of hearing that her husband was "off the reservation," as she put it, she just couldn't tell her pastor, for what would he think? And she did not want anyone in town to know that her marriage was in danger of breaking up.

From the lady's story it appeared that she and her husband had been childhood sweethearts and had met in the kindergarten class in Sunday school. Their families, near-neighbors, were workers in the church—good, solid Christian people. When George and Alice were married, they moved to a nearby medium-sized city where, ultimately, they became owners of a construction company. She handled the office, he the outside work, and they worked together as a closely-knit team. "And while we worked long hours and had many problems, still, we had lots of fun, too!" she said, remembering. They made a fair income and had a nice home, but Alice continued to do the housework and cook the meals.

Then in quick succession two children came along, which kept Alice at home. A clerk was hired to do her job at the office. Alice soon became frazzled with the housework and the children, and she missed the former camaraderie and the interesting world of business. When George came home, he acted tired and grumpy and was highly critical of his wife and her handling of home affairs. They had very little social life, although, as it now appeared, George was having some on his own. Needless to say, they had drifted away from churchgoing.

"Now, Alice," I said, "keep your cool going, and when George comes home have a quiet talk with him— and underscore *quiet*; no hysterics. And start praying right now. Don't feverishly implore God to help you, but quietly thank Him for doing so. For He *is* helping you, right now. Turn this situation over to the power of Jesus Christ. He has His own way of handling things. Then see if you can persuade George to telephone me. Tell him that you and I have already talked, and I will keep you both in my prayers."

THE HUSBAND TELEPHONES
A day or two later the husband telephoned. A quiet voice said, "This is George ——— from ———. I want to apologize for my wife's bothering you."

"Oh, that is what I am here for," I replied, "to help anyone I can. I am glad to hear from you. Just what is the situation?"

"Oh, I love Alice very much, of course I do. I always have since we were kids. But, Dr. Peale, she just doesn't keep up. She is a very pretty girl, but she has let herself get to looking like the wrath of God. I even saw her going into a supermarket with curlers in her hair. And I've just got to say that she is a lousy housekeeper. The place is in a perpetual mess. She can be a terrific cook when she wants to, but apparently she never wants to, for she throws the stuff on the table, and never in the dining room but in the kitchen, with pots and pans stacked high in the sink. And the food—well, we might as well eat at McDonald's—never anything but hamburger and more hamburger. But the worst of it is, she just doesn't seem to understand my problems anymore. I can't ever talk to her."

"And now you have found someone who does understand and sympathize—is that it?"

"Well," he declared, "it is just a friendship, someone to talk to. There is no emotional involvement."

"It seems to me you've allowed your wife to become a sort of galley slave. I wonder if you ever help her around the house, and why not loosen up and hire a maid?"

"She doesn't want one, and besides, none are to be had in our town. And about helping her! When I come home from work I've had it; what I need is to relax."

"She probably needs to relax, also," I murmured.

"Yeah, maybe so," he admitted.

"George," I said, "I've got to tell you that you can be headed for trouble, lots of trouble. And this so-called 'friend' can be playing you for all you're worth. I understand you and your wife met in Sunday school, from which you have wandered away. Just as a suggestion, how about talking this matter over with the Man you met in Sunday school? He is pretty well up on such situations as the one you are getting into."

"Who's that?" asked George.

"Jesus Christ," I replied.

"Guess you're right, doctor; yes, you could be right. I'll give it some thought." So saying, he hung up.

Soon thereafter I telephoned his wife. "Look," I said, "I have some advice for you. And please don't ask me why—just follow it and I have a feeling we can handle your situation, you and I and the Lord." Then I made a suggestion that certainly startled her, but she listened without expressing surprise. I told her to go out and get some well-styled new clothes and, with them, a hairdo, and start always appearing neat and well-dressed during the day and then in late afternoon put on a long dress. Then she was to set the table, using her best silver and dishes, together with candles. The house was to be tidied up as though company were expected.

The first result of this was that George ran into Alice downtown. "Why all the glad rags?" he growled.

"Look pretty nice, don't I?" said his wife. Then George, coming home in the late afternoon, found Alice perfectly coiffured, in a long dress, laying out the table ceremoniously. He showed surprise but made no comment, and went out slamming the door a bit louder than necessary.

Alice, perfectly gowned, sat down to a lonely candle-light dinner when suddenly the front door banged open and George came rushing in. "Who are you waiting for here?" he demanded angrily.

"I'm waiting for the nicest man in the world, the one I love with all my heart," said Alice with smiling face. George stood, bewildered, conflicting emotions passing over his countenance. "You're not meeting someone?" he persisted.

"Only you," Alice answered, "always and forever only you. I want to tell you that you have a new wife. The old one had grown quite shabby. And no other girl is ever going to get you away from me. With the Lord's help I can beat her at her own game."

George stood uncertainly, then a look of admiration was followed by a huge relieved laugh. "Do you know something, honey?" he said. "There's no one like you, no one at all. I love you; I really do. Come on, dish up dinner. It must be a good one."

"Now, George, no such plebian talk. I'll call you when dinner is served, sir."

At dinner George said, "How did you think this one up, honey? I knew you were smart, and . . . and . . . " He seemed choked up. "You really love me, don't you?" She nodded through tears. "I guess I'd forgotten. I've been irritated, thoughtless, and mean." He jumped up, ran the length of the table, lifted her up in his arms, bear-hugging her. "What a dope I've been, what a dope! No one can touch you, do you hear what I say? No one is in your league, absolutely no one—and I mean no one at all." Then he sat silently thinking. "I know what happened. You prayed to Jesus and that's how you got this idea of dressing up and the candlelight and everything."

"That's right, George. Jesus brought us together in the first place, and Jesus will always keep us together."

"You said it, sweetheart," agreed George. The positive power of Jesus Christ had worked another miracle in an era when marriages come apart with such seeming ease—another amazing result of the power.

HE FOUND HIMSELF

The problem of so many persons is that of never finding themselves. In youth this failure is understandable, for youth can be a period of confusion and experimentation, an often unhappy era in one's experience. But when successive years go by and one is still trying to find himself as a person, to know his own identity, to discover purpose and meaning, the problem becomes ever more complex and results in dissatisfaction and, of course, an unhappy attitude toward the self.

Then it is that God, in His own astonishing way, finds such a person and enters deeply into his consciousness. The result is that the individual has the experience of self-revelation. He finds himself with clarity and understanding so that his life, coming finally under effective divine control, uses powers and abilities that are consolidated and focused, and he becomes an effective person.

Such was the personal experience of a man down South, who wrote me the letter that follows:

Dear Dr. Peale:

One hot summer night in 1964 when my life was at an all-time low I wandered into a newsstand not really knowing what I was looking for. A bright, shiny red cover on your paperback of *The Power of Positive Thinking* caught my attention. At that time I hadn't been in church for five or six years.

I'm confident that you have heard many similar experiences and that my story is not really extra-special except to me. However, I will be ever grateful to you for the wonderful things that have happened these past fourteen years. You have helped me achieve a wonderful relationship with God and He has blessed me in so many ways. The greatest blessing being His Son Jesus Christ.

Dr. Peale, I was a complete failure at the time you came into my life. My marriage had just broken up. I was a college dropout and I was a low-paid employee. With God's help I started my way back to being the kind of person that God wanted me to be. Now I will be the first to say that I still have a great way to go, but "I can do all things through Christ that strengthens me."[4]

To show you how bad my attitude was, my own father had to give me a failing grade in a class that I had him for in high school. My first college experience was a series of incompletes and failing grades. The first job that I had paid only $225 a month. After nearly five years I had advanced to a little over $300 a month and no real change in responsibility.

Within a week after finding your book, things really started to change. Christ became the guiding light in my life. The progress has been a steady series of advances and setbacks, but the theme has always been positive and the direction has been ever upward. The Sunday after I started reading your book I was back in church with my godlike and understanding parents. My break with God had been so complete I'm embarrassed to say that I had to learn the Lord's Prayer over again.

Dr. Peale, with the motivation you gave me, I started to look for a college that I could return to. With the help of some fine educators it was determined that I had average ability, and that if I was fortunate to find a school that would take my grades from my original college I probably could finish an undergraduate program in business. Several college admission officers refused me a chance. And one in particular was very negative about my chances. My response to him was a strong positive assurance that I was not only going to complete my college degree, but I was also going to complete my Master's degree as well. When he said that it would not be at his college because he could not take a chance on me, I simply smiled and told him that it might not be at his college, but I was positive it would happen. To this day I remember him looking me in the eye and saying, "You know, with an attitude like yours, it probably will."

4. Philippians 4:13

He was right. With God's help I not only returned to college to complete my undergraduate work on the Dean's List, I was also blessed with a fellowship to help me complete my Master's in Business Administration.

From this great experience God led me to my beautiful wife. Within two months a year later, God gave me even more than I ever dreamed of. She and I were married, with His help I successfully completed my M.B.A. exams and degree, and He led me to a corporation where I have been employed ever since. The good Lord has given me a unique opportunity to witness to Christ in the business world. In less than ten years with this company I have been blessed with eight different responsibilities. Each time He has asked me to do more and each time He has given me more.

During this time God has given my wife and me two beautiful children. Today, Dr. Peale, I have so many blessings it would take hours to discuss them all. The greatest of all is God and His Son, Jesus. Because of you I am with Christ. Prayer and thanksgiving are part of my daily life. Church is very important, and like the air I breathe each day I'm fortunate to have an opportunity to be part of a wonderful church and serve as an officer.

Maybe someday we can meet again. You have done so much for so many. Meeting you recently and hearing you speak was a great spiritual uplift. My experience of meeting you has prompted me into giving a witness to Christ.

God bless you, Dr. Peale.

6

Faith and the Power

FAITH IS A VITAL, LIFE-CHANGING, AND CREATIVE power in human experience. It is belief in and intellectual assent to valid doctrine and acceptance of a sound theological position. But even more, faith is an in-depth assurance, a profound certainty that God will actually do what, in the Bible, He says He will do. The promises of Holy Scripture I personally believe to be true, without any doubt whatsoever.

So the reason for my strong faith is that the Bible teaches faith. Faith has demonstrated its validity in all kinds of circumstances in my life. As I have believed and practiced faith in God and in Jesus Christ, the most wonderful things have happened: peace, joy, and victory. Moreover, other people with deep faith, known to me, have experienced, unmistakably, the power of God operating in their lives. As a result, my own faith in faith as the power of God in action has become ever more certain. As St. Paul says, "I am not ashamed of the gospel of Christ: for it is the power of God unto salvation to every one that believeth."[1]

The New Testament contains some very strong assertions about the power of faith. For example, there is the incident of the two blind men who received their sight because they believed: "And when Jesus departed thence, two blind men followed him, crying, and saying, Thou Son of David, have mercy on us. And when he was come into the house, the blind men came to him: and Jesus saith unto them, Believe ye that I am able to do this? They said unto him, Yea, Lord. Then touched he their eyes, saying, According to your faith be it unto you. And their eyes were opened."[2]

1. Romans 1:16   2. Matthew 9:27–30

Again the Bible tells us that by faith we can move mountains of difficulty and trouble. "Verily I say unto you, If ye have faith as a grain of mustard seed, ye shall say unto this mountain, Remove hence to yonder place; and it shall remove: and nothing shall be impossible unto you."[3] This means no superficial or soft kind of faith, but instead the kind that makes and keeps us "strong and of a good courage."[4] It must be real, deep, positive faith. The sturdy, faith-believing, wonder-working New Testament tells us, "I can do all things through Christ which strengtheneth me."[5]

HE BELIEVED FAITH HAS POWER

No doubt some Christians "sort of" believe in the foregoing passages of Scripture, but from the standpoint of actually living upon them, they are hardly prepared to accept them as actual. But my friend Bob Case was made of sterner stuff. He believed, and for sure, with no room mentally for rationalization. He had forthright faith as stated in the Scripture quoted above.

Bob lived in Syracuse, New York, where he was a dynamic and completely convinced member of my church. He had come into the faith via a definite spiritual, life-changing experience. He became a student of the Bible on his own and furthered his understanding by attendance at a Bible class taught by an outstanding Bible scholar. He joined the New York State Police, a superior body of men chosen for their high character and personality traits. He was an impressive specimen of man-

3. Matthew 17:20   4. Joshua 1:9   5. Philippians 4:13

hood, powerfully built physically, and endowed with mental equipment of high order. Indeed, he had the makings of a scholar and impressed some faculty people in the Syracuse University community as being an unusual thinker. But he liked the outdoor life of a state policeman and was committed to public service in upholding law and order. Not a few young people were saved from erring ways by this upstanding and caring police officer.

But Bob's chief characteristic was faith in Christ—unalloyed, definite, positive faith. He was a believer in depth. His faith was based upon mental search and reason. He moved up into a mental area of belief that was beyond the doubt that often waters down faith. He accepted Christ and His teachings because he believed this to be the way of truth.

When I left Syracuse to begin my ministry in New York, I gradually lost touch with Bob. Then one night years later I went to Kingston, New York, to fill a speaking engagement. I took a train to Poughkeepsie, having been informed that someone would meet me at the station and transport me some eighteen miles to Kingston and return me afterward to Poughkeepsie for a train back to New York City.

To my surprise when I stepped off the train at Poughkeepsie, who should be on the platform but my old friend Bob Case. He explained that he now lived in Kingston and had volunteered to be my chauffeur. Naturally we had a great visit about old times, but it was his own personal story that gripped me and resulted in a new input of faith into my own experience. It was the story of a believer with a powerful faith, a positive faith.

ACCIDENT WHILE PURSUING A CRIMINAL

One night, in the line of duty, Bob was pursuing an escaping criminal down Route 9, then a winding, narrow road alongside the Hudson River. The escapee was in a car; Bob, the state policeman, on a motorcycle. The criminal gunned the car to high speed, at times approaching one hundred miles an hour, but Bob held closely upon the speeding car. His job was to apprehend the man and, faithful to his sworn duty, Bob took chances with his own safety in this hair-raising chase.

It was wintertime and there were spots of glare ice on the road, some of them hidden under a light dusting of snow. At a turn Bob's motorcycle struck one of these icy spots at an angle. The machine went out of control, slid across the road, hurtled over a ditch, plowed through a fence, and threw Bob into a stubbled cornfield, where he lay seemingly dead.

He was picked up by an ambulance and taken to a hospital where, miraculously, except for bruises he was found to be uninjured, and in a day or two was released. But some weeks later, when he started to get up, to his amazement he found that he could barely move; it was as if his body was partially frozen tight. His wife attempted to lift him, but because he was such a big man and a dead weight, she was unable to move him. She summoned the doctor who, upon examination, diagnosed the trouble as a form of latent arthritis which had apparently been activated by the violence of the spill from the motorcycle. "Lie still a day or so while we give you treatment," said the doctor.

Came a day when the doctor, sitting by the patient's bed, attempted in the most careful and diplomatic manner to convey to Bob that, from the best medical point of view, he was likely to be an invalid. Indeed, the doctor expressed the opinion that it was unlikely he would be able to walk. He did leave some vestige of hope that long therapy might possibly be helpful. Meanwhile he would just have to adjust mentally to a restricted situation.

Bob looked up at the doctor with a smile. "Doc," he said, "you're my friend and I like you. I realize how hard it is for you to tell a big, strong, active man that he is through. I understand what you are really saying through all those kind words. And I will faithfully take your medicine and your therapy. But, Doc, I have another Doctor besides you and I've been talking to Him and remembering how He healed the lame, the halt, and the blind. And I'm lame and halt, and I remembered that it was said of Him that He is 'the same yesterday, and today, and for ever.'[6] So if you don't mind, I'm going to ask Him for healing." The doctor stood looking at his patient, then suddenly put his hand on his head. "You're a great guy, Bob," he said. "And about that Doctor you mention; He and I work together." And he went away on his rounds.

Next morning Bob called his wife. "Go get Bill and Jack and bring them in here."

"What are you going to do?" asked his wife in alarm.

"I'm going to get up and walk," he replied calmly. "And don't you worry, Jesus will help me." More persuasion was necessary, but seeing that her husband was determined and well knowing the simplicity and strength of his faith, she called in the two strong neighbors. "Lift me up and set me on my feet, boys," said Bob, "and stand by to steady me for a moment."

It was a heavy job, but they got Bob to his feet where

6. Hebrews 13:8

he tottered shakily, but his legs held him up. Slowly, aided by a man on either side, he shuffled forward. "It's just like the man by the pool: 'Take up thy bed, and walk,'"[7] said the patient, with glowing face.

"Yeah," said Jack, "but, Bob, that was in the Bible about a man a long while ago. Better be careful."

"Oh, no, Jack, the Lord also meant me when He spoke to that fellow in the Bible."

At Kingston I made my speech, after which Bob drove me back to the Poughkeepsie station. Standing with him on the platform I said, "Tell you what, walk up and down so I can see just how well you do." Sturdily he walked up and down, lifting his feet in rhythm. Aside from a bit of a limp in the left leg, all seemed normal. Then I asked, "But don't you ever suffer pain?" A big smile overspread his face. "Pain? Sure, I have pain, plenty of it. But, you see, that is part of the deal. And I can take it because Jesus helps me bear it. Just to walk was enough to ask of Him."

The train rushed into the station, heavily laden with upstate snow which swirled all about us. Quickly we shook hands. "God bless you, old boy," I said, deeply moved.

"He always does," he replied.

The train started to move and I waved to him as he stood in the glow of the platform lights. He waved back and I saw him walk along with the train for a moment before we passed out of sight. "What a man!" I thought, "what a man!" One of the great, strong men Christ makes. What I had seen was the impressive greatness of the believer, an enormous demonstration of faith and the power.

7. John 5:11

The foregoing case history quite definitely indicates that when belief is held firmly and adhered to with a minimum or complete absence of doubt, forces are released which produce remarkable results; the ancients would have called them miracles. Indeed, they may still be that in fact, though now we are more familiar with the scientific mental operations involved in bringing great happenings, that is to say, miracles, to pass. It is a demonstrated fact that the rugged and convinced believer sends forth from his mind and his spirit emanations of power or strong forces inherent in personality which make it possible for God to do wonders and achieve results which are truly extraordinary.

HE FACED A DEAD END

Many letters come to me from people, especially from youth, telling how, through positive faith in Christ and by the process of positive thinking, they have been able to surmount the most appalling difficulties and overcome great odds. They describe coming to seeming dead ends, with all hope for the future vanished. Then, through an increase of faith in God, commitment to Christ, and positive thinking, they have found a way to make their dreams come true.

Such was the experience of Gilbert, a young man from West Africa, who wrote me the victorious letter which follows:

> I was doing my last year in the high school in a small town, Buea, in Cameroon, in West Africa. That year was not only my last year in the high school, but also the year when I started seeing the rays of the sun of hope. It was the year I rose from fear to faith, the year that life started to have a meaning for me, the year I

found my Saviour, and all because it was the year I read your book *The Power of Positive Thinking*. After reading that book my life took on a new dimension. In a nutshell, this is my story.

I was about to drop out of school, not because I could not take my lessons nor because I hated schooling, but rather because my parents could not pay my fees even though I was on partial scholarship. There was nothing before me but an empty future. I was balanced on a high peak of need, agonized by indecision.

One day, after a short period of conversation with a friend, he promised and did bring me this book. At first I could not believe what it was saying, for it was too good to be true. Moreover, I have never heard of such a philosophy before, quite different from what I had heard and seen practiced. It was strange in "my world."

But I had to accept it because there was no other alternative, for as the saying goes, once down, there is but one direction, upwards. Every line I read brought a new dream into my soul and an eradication of an old doubt. I made up my mind to do away with whatever I had previously believed, if possible my own name. The first thing I did after reading it was to send it to my brother and made him promise to read it and get as many of our friends as possible to read it, as I was in the boarding house and could not do it myself. I was so carried away by this philosophy that when I came on holiday, peers simply called me the power of positive thinking. I not only preached it then but practiced it as well. I no longer cared how my fee was going to be paid and till today I can't explain how it was. I just simply believed it would be paid and surely it was paid.

My first and major goal was to continue my education to university level. I told myself that I was not only going to go to a university but to go to a university in America. I proclaimed this so strongly that some of my friends started doubting my sanity. I ignored them and just started doing the things I could do, like applying to schools for admission. Two days before my departure,

I just walked to a friend and asked him for money to buy my flight ticket and he did so without questioning. God is just wonderful. I praise His holy name. Dr. Peale, it has been story after story since that time.

Tomorrow will make me two years in this country. For these two years I have been constantly in school even though I entered into this country with less than two hundred dollars. I am fully equipped, for I have my God and my faith in Him through Christ. I must succeed.

I am no longer afraid of tomorrow, for I know that He is the God of yesterday, today, and forevermore.

Sir, I can't thank you well enough. You helped lift me up and by God's grace I shall stay there.

Thanks a lot, Dr. Peale.

This young man, with practically nothing at all in the way of financial resources or human help, moved out on faith alone. And this action, which most "practical" persons would regard as foolhardy, led him to a university halfway across the world. Money can exercise power, friends can create power, but the quiet and seemingly incredible power of faith, when it takes hold completely as it did in this instance, becomes superior to all other forms of power. Again and always the Scriptural statement is true: "If ye have faith as a grain of mustard seed . . . [even as small as that, but real] . . . nothing shall be impossible unto you."[8] This is not fantasy. It is verifiable fact demonstrated in persons every day, as it was in the story contained in the foregoing letter.

Furthermore, the positive power of faith operates as a releasing agent of the potential inherent in a person. The young man from West Africa discovered within himself qualities, abilities, forces of which he was only

8. Matthew 17:20

vaguely aware, if indeed he was aware of them at all. The excitement of a new thought pattern stimulated by the book *The Power of Positive Thinking*, a philosophy totally new to him, dramatically activated powers which had been dormant within but exploded when tapped. But they exploded under definite, enthusiastic direction. The direction came from Jesus Christ, to whom this boy looked for guidance.

When we consider the built-in possibilities in human nature we should recall a great statement of Thomas A. Edison to the effect that if we were to do all the things we are capable of doing, we would literally astonish ourselves. Have you ever really astonished yourself? That question deserves soul-searching. The positive power, when let loose through faith, brings out the most astonishing qualities in people, often capacities hitherto unsuspected.

LIBERAL OR CONSERVATIVE

As one of those reared and trained in a scientific tradition and in the intellectual atmosphere of universities, I am grateful that at the same time I remained rooted in the faith pattern of those everyday, down-to-earth, spiritually committed, salt-of-the-earth Americans. Some religious leaders have a tendency to become enthralled with every new concept that comes along, and describe it as "an insight from the best minds of our time." Then they talk about it, push it, glorify it to the extent that to question it is at the peril of being considered "out of it." Such ideas change from time to time, but always the "this is it" attitude prevails and the "take it or else" threat compels many to go along. Almost always, belief in and commitment to Jesus Christ is minimized.

As to my own spiritual history, I was born in an era of simple faith and was brought up in an area of strong evangelical emphasis. I was taught to believe in God, in Christ, in the Holy Spirit, in conversion, holiness, re-generation, resurrection, and life after death. I was taught that God could and would do wonderful things in my life and, if it was His will, bless others through me. In a word, I was reared to walk humbly with my God and believe implicitly in His Son, Jesus Christ my Savior.

Then came a call to the ministry, which was resolutely resisted. Having spent my boyhood as a minister's son, I was not about to be for all my life under the supervision of the church. I loved God and Jesus and the church, but wanted a "normal" life, that of a layman. In fact, being a bit fed up with the church hierarchy, especially so-called church leaders who seemed to have all the answers, I wanted to think out my own solutions and work with my own ideas and believe as I personally wanted to believe. Certainly no theological professor or board secretary or far-out preacher was going to tell me what my religion should be. To know Christ for myself in my own way was my objective. He was my own Savior and my relationship with Him was my own; it was meaningful and sacred to me. If it wasn't up-to-date, modern, and in the latest mode, that was my business, and I meant to keep it that way.

But then, finally, being no longer able to hold out against what I humbly felt to be the Lord's call to serve Him in the ministry, I entered Boston University Graduate School, though not the Theological Department. It was strange how I kept shying off from going all-out for the ministry. In the graduate school I registered for a couple of courses in theology which were to be credited toward a Master of Arts degree. In this experimentation came the discovery that the boys in the theological school were regular good fellows and the professors were highly competent and thoughtful. Indeed, they were so intellectually stimulating that entrance into theological education was no longer resisted. Then began the process of reeducating my "simple" faith, as it was rather amazingly referred to. I became an enthusiastic, all-out exponent of the "social gospel," the "in" point of view at the time. It taught that Christianity is a social manifesto for change in society's structure. However, I never did agree with the idea put forth by some that other social systems are superior to free enterprise under the American way. I did believe that one purpose of Christianity is the development of a better world for all men, but certainly never shared in the concept attributed to the then current Christian leadership by a newspaper writer that "to be a Christian is to call a strike."

During my years at Boston University I was sufficiently "in" to be considered a follower of "the party line," which meant complete adherence to the current theological mode. At the same time, my long-held conviction that Christianity is also a technique for personal life change, and that the power of faith creatively works in us as individuals, was never in any sense reduced. Therefore I was considered a mixture of what was called liberal and conservative. Those were rather definite and exact descriptive labels at that time. But my, shall we say, "liberalism" was never at any period as strong as my conservativism. The latter had much deeper roots in my personal beliefs.

My natural scientific slant of mind finally led me into the effort to unify Christian pastoral functions cooperatively with psychological medicine. I became a pioneer in establishing the fact that the pastor and the psychiatrist were natural partners—that they could work together, each respecting the other's identity and function, but cooperatively pooling their resources to help normal people live normal lives.

The American Foundation of Religion and Psychiatry, which I established jointly with the noted psychiatrist Dr. Smiley Blanton, was the first organization that firmly established a working relationship between religion and psychiatry. It developed into a therapy of vast importance both to the church and to psychiatry. In fact, to this organization goes the credit for breaking down a longtime hostility that had existed between religion and psychiatry. It pointed the way for a new and exciting creative partnership. In our joint work people were healed of emotional ills primarily by faith, the greatest of all therapies. Further, psychiatry helped us, as pastors, better to understand and deal with the complexities of the human mind, where the inner conflicts of personality illnesses occur and with which the pastor is called upon to deal.

More than anything I ever learned in any school was the insight into human beings taught me by Dr. Blanton. "A Tennessee hillbilly Methodist," as he loved to term himself, he was a man of deep, old-fashioned faith. Yet, at the same time, he was a student and close associate of Dr. Sigmund Freud of Vienna and was profoundly versed in Freud's emphasis on the sense of guilt and the powerful effect upon human behavior of the deep unconscious, or subconscious. Dr. Blanton combined, in a remarkable working unity, his old-fashioned religious faith and his modern scientific methodology. After applying the latter to a patient, he would often say to me, "Now, Norman, just give him the good old gospel."

I once asked Dr. Blanton what were the basic requirements for being a successful psychiatrist. At once he answered, "Insight and love." Insight, he pointed out, is the ability to see into, to practice empathy with, a patient. It is an intuitive perceptiveness or understanding of what goes on in the mind. Dr. Blanton said, "You either have insight or you do not. You cannot go to college and have it taught to you. No university has a chair of insight. If you possess native insight, the quality may be developed and enhanced, but basically it is a gift of God." So he believed.

The second needed quality, he told me, is love. The doctor must love the disturbed and distraught person who comes for help. No matter how badly the patient may react, hatefully or even violently, one must project to him or her compassionate, loving thoughts, because, he said, "Love heals; it always heals." With this point of view, Dr. Blanton had to be a man of faith, as indeed he was. Guilt was healed by faith in Christ, in his view. The love of Christ was the love with which he treated a patient. "There is no gap," he asserted, "between scientific methodology and the gospel, for the gospel is itself a science. Live by the precise formulas laid down in the great rule book, the Bible, and the result will be a healthy, normal and happy person."

MY EAR IS HEALED

The fact that my own belief has long been a combination of faith and science was demonstrated in an interesting experience. A few years ago I went back to my native

Ohio for an anniversary occasion in the little town of Bowersville, my birthplace. This is located some twenty miles from Dayton, in Greene County. Bowersville had a population of perhaps 350 when I was born and is still a very small village, but one of the most beautiful to be found anywhere, at least to my nostalgic eyes. This celebration was held in the high school auditorium, and there was a capacity crowd on hand.

In the afternoon my left ear began to pain me considerably. As a boy I used to suffer from earaches, but hadn't had one for many years. On the way to Bowersville from Dayton the earache became worse, until the pain was quite excruciating. When we arrived at the high school I told my wife Ruth, "Please go in and tell the people in charge that I am here but to go ahead with the program; that I am having a little trouble with my ear and will remain in the car until needed. When the time comes for me to speak, come out and get me and I will try to pull myself together enough to make my speech. But keep the meeting going as long as possible before coming back!"

Sitting in the car, suffering with this intense earache, I practiced all the positive thinking I could muster. It was impossible to imagine why this earache had come upon me, for no such experience had happened since boyhood. Suddenly there came a tap on the window of the car. I rolled it down and a man said, "Have you an earache?"

"Yes, sir," I replied, "I do indeed."

"Well, I am only a farmer, but the Lord has given me the power to heal in some cases. I am not a doctor, and I am not a crank—just a simple believer to whom this gift has been granted. May I try to cure that earache of yours with the Lord's help?"

"Please, go ahead. What am I to do?"

"All you do is have faith," he assured me. "Within every human being are all the curative resources needed for healing. When a physical problem arises, it is because the curative resources have been depreciated."

"You mean I have the resources within me to cure this earache?"

"That is right," he replied, "if you will believe and if you will so affirm." He was a big fellow, obviously an earnest, dedicated Christian man, and I liked him. I believed in him, too. He put his hands over both my ears and said, "Now go to work spiritually."

"I thought *you* were going to do the work," I said pointedly.

"We must both work together. You are to visualize the creative resources of health within you and talk to God in prayer. Affirm His healing grace." I really went to work to visualize the healing powers at work. After a while I began to feel better. The ache eased remarkably; the pain was definitely reduced. I thanked the man. "God made the ear," he said, "and He can correct it when it is not working right."

Then a doctor of medicine came along and said, "I have heard you are suffering from earache."

"Yes, but you're too late. I feel much better. A man who is a faith healer has helped me greatly."

"Well . . . " the doctor countered, as he pulled out his needle, "even so, we'll give you a shot in the arm."

I went ahead with my speech and did so with only a faint feeling in the ear. Next morning the pain was gone altogether, and I have never had an earache since.

You may take your choice as to who performed the healing, the faith healer or the doctor of medicine. I am inclined to credit both. But I never forgot that kindly, plain-spoken farmer who gently put his big, rough hands on my ears and told me the great fact that Almighty God has built great health resources into every individual. Whether it is a problem of health or any other kind of problem, faith in Him is equal to it. The important fact to realize is that God can bring to your aid the resources He put within you and which you may never have tapped. What a combination: scientific faith and faith-motivated science!

The important point to be underscored is that faith is an expression of actual power, a positive power that can and regularly does produce the most amazing results in the lives of people when they cast aside doubts and believe, *really* believe. These are not always dramatic events, but are significant occurrences in the lives of plain, simple people, as in the case of my ear.

SHE BELIEVED HER BABY WOULD BE PERFECT

One such incident is that of a young wife about to become a mother. She was young but strong in her faith, and she fell back upon the positive power of Jesus Christ in a major crisis. Nor did it fail her. This is her letter to me:

Dear Dr. Peale,

About a year ago, I gave birth to our first child. The pregnancy was easy, but two months before delivery the doctor told me the baby was breech and there was no room for her to turn around. The doctor said he had confidence that he could deliver this breech baby properly.

As it turned out, during labor her chin became caught on the pelvic bone. The doctors pulled frantically to get her out, and a nerve in her neck became damaged. The pulled nerve resulted in paralysis on her right side.

She was immediately rushed to Children's Hospital. Things looked dim. The intern told me she would probably have an enlarged head.

I was reading your *Power of Positive Thinking* book at the time. I took your advice. I stayed calm. I prayed every day. Then I put it in God's hands. But the whole time, I had faith that she would be healed. Real faith. I sat next to her incubator and prayed. Everyone said, "How can Mary be so calm?" I just believed, that's all.

Well, she got a little better each day, with the help of some medicine. After the ninth day, I walked into the hospital room and the nurse said, "Oh, Mrs. Robertson, Nicole can be released today." Thank God!

Nicole is a very healthy and normal little girl—with no enlarged head.

Thank the Lord.

An altogether different type of person was the man who was my seatmate on a flight to St. Louis. He spoke pleasantly, then opened his briefcase, took out some papers, and went to work. Having some paper work to do myself, I realized gratefully that here was a man who would not waste time in idle conversation. When one has work to do, people who just want to visit can, however nice, become a bit of a problem.

Then, to my surprise, the man took a Bible from his briefcase and began to read. There were bits of paper marking certain pages and one by one he read the indicated references. Finally he closed the Bible and sat back in an attitude of meditation. After a short period he resumed his work but seemed to be making some kind of a list. When he finished the list he folded the paper and placed it in the pocket of his shirt. Then he put all his work away, seemingly finished, picked up the airline magazine, and started to read.

My curiosity was so aroused that I said, "My friend, I'm interested to see you reading marked places in the Bible, and apparently doing it with some sort of system. I happen to be a pastor, and if it isn't being nosy, would appreciate knowing if you employ some special method in Bible reading."

"You say you are a pastor. May I ask your name?" When I told him he said, "I thought I'd seen you somewhere. You spoke at my industry convention once. If my method can be helpful to someone else, certainly I will be glad to share it, but I don't want any particular credit for it." I promised not to use his name if I ever told about our conversation.

METHOD FOR USING THE POWER IN CRISIS
"I happen to be facing a crisis at this time," went on my seatmate. "Just what it is is irrelevant, but to get ready for it my mind must be working at maximum, so I follow a five-point procedure. First, I sharpen my mind by reading St. Paul. In my opinion, next to Jesus, his was the keenest mind in history. So I read St. Paul to sharpen my mind on his, as a farmer whets a scythe on a grindstone."

"I knew a man in New York who did the same thing," I said, "and he was an extraordinary thinker."

"That is what I'm trying to become." He continued. "Second, the marked places you noticed are verses that have to do with faith. In facing the upcoming crisis I need faith as well as the ability to think coherently. Having memorized these verses, I practice letting them soak into my conscious mind, seeping finally into the subconscious. That is not original with me. As a matter of fact, that idea came from one of your books," he acknowledged.

"Thanks," I replied. "It's a sound idea."

"Sure is," he agreed. "That is why I use it. But even though I have these Scripture statements memorized, I find that it helps now and then to read them again from the Book itself. It sort of reinforces their authority.

"Then you may have noticed that I leaned back in a relaxed manner and closed my eyes." I nodded. "That is my third step. I affirm God's presence. I remind myself that the Lord is with me, for He said: 'I am with you always.'[9] I spend a moment sensing and feeling the Lord's actual presence. And I assure you that is a very real fact to me. When you really believe in the Presence, then the Presence is there, and for sure. At least, that is the way I find it.

"Next, I pray that my decisions will be right, for I know that if a decision isn't right it's wrong, and that nothing wrong ever turns out right.

"Finally, and my fifth step, I visualize and image a good outcome of this crisis. I form a mental picture of how I think it should be. I am now holding that image or pictured outcome in consciousness, knowing that what we strongly image tends to be reproduced in fact.

"Having completed those five procedures, I then practice one of the wisest bits of advice in the Bible. Know what that is?"

"You tell me," I urged.

"'Having done all, to stand.'[10] When you've done all you can do, what more can you do? Just put everything confidently into God's hands. He will bring it out O.K.

9. Matthew 28:20   10. Ephesians 6:13

Finally, I put this list in my shirt pocket to keep faith close to my heart."

What a commonsense and highly practical technique for meeting crisis.

Power, the positive power of faith, operates as God wills it in the crisis experiences of people as illustrated by the young mother and the business executive. They both had simple faith, or, shall we say, they had strong faith uncomplicated.

A weak or doubtful expression of faith has little or no power to affect people other than to turn them off. But a strong, believing witness expressed with certainty and positive conviction strongly persuades and wins men and women to acceptance. Indeed, a definite assertion of belief in God, in Christ and the great teachings of the Christian faith could exert such power as to turn the world from moral deterioration to a new era of morality that would rival the greatest spiritual movements of history.

In my ministry I have found that nonpracticing Christians, nonchurchgoers, the irreligious, and even those who are actively hostile to Christianity will listen with respect to a person who forthrightly expresses his faith, who shows no doubt or sounds no uncertain note, provided it is done with intelligence and control and with kindness. I have personally won many people to Christ and the church by not hesitating to voice a positive faith and witnessing to it with conviction both in public and privately in one-to-one relationships.

HE WANTED A STRAIGHT ANSWER
A telephone message came that Mr. Alfred P. Sloan, the industrialist who had much to do with the creation of

the General Motors Corporation and who was then its president, "desperately" wanted to see me. This seemed strange to me, never having met Mr. Sloan. But it was explained that his wife of fifty years, to whom he was utterly devoted, had died, and he was desolated. No one had been able to give him any peace or comfort, and, being a reader of my books, he had now turned to me for help. He was so depressed that he was not leaving his house, and the caller asked if I would be good enough to call upon him at his home in New York City.

Mr. Sloan was an impressive figure and a dominant personality. He had a rather stern facial expression and a direct, businesslike manner. He fixed a cool, direct gaze on me, looking out of eyes that brooked no evasiveness. "I want to ask you a simple question," he said, "and I don't want any weasel answer or philosophical discussion. I want a straightforward, unequivocal yes or no. I want an answer, and if you don't know it, say so." I gave him as straight and firm a look as he leveled at me. "O.K., you ask a straight question and I will give you a straight answer," I said.

"Here's what I want to know. My wife recently died. I loved my wife and depended upon her. When I die will I be with my wife again? Now," he continued, "I called in a curate from a nearby church and put this question to him. He gave me a lot of inconclusive gobbledygook and actually came up with a sort of muttering that we take a more educated and modern look at such things as immortality in this enlightened day and age. I got rid of him as soon as I could. He was a not-dry-behind-the-ears kind of guy. Now, what's *your* answer?"

"The answer is yes."

"How sure are you?"

"Absolutely, positively 100 percent sure."

In a sense I was amazed by the almost childlikeness of this great man, though outwardly he gave the impression of dominance and power. He explained that his wife had possessed a great brain and intuitive knowledge of people, the ability to reason. "I bounced all my ideas off her mind," he said, "and she came up with remarkable insights." He struggled with his emotion. "She was my life. To her I came home every evening. She was my home. Whatever will I do without her?" Tears stood in his eyes; his voice trembled. But he shook off the emotion. "So you're absolutely sure? Why?"

I proceeded to tell him the reason for my certainty: that the Bible clearly teaches life after death for those who love the Lord and have experienced His grace. I quoted such passages as "Because I live, ye shall live also,"[11] and again, "I am the resurrection, and the life: he that believeth in me, though he were dead, yet shall he live: And whosoever liveth and believeth in me shall never die."[12] I reminded him of how Jesus appeared to many and that His own resurrection had impeccable proof; I reminded him that "in him we live, and move, and have our being."[13] I gave him every Biblical assurance that came to mind at the moment.

Then I added, "Mr. Sloan, to be sure that you will meet your wife in eternal life, that quality of life must be in you. Tell me, then, your identification with this verse of Scripture: 'And this is the record, that God hath given to us eternal life, and this life is in his Son. He that hath the Son hath life; and he that hath not the Son of God hath not life. These things have I written unto

11. John 14:19   12. John 11:25, 26   13. Acts 17:28

you that believe on the name of the Son of God; that ye may know that ye have eternal life, and that ye may believe on the name of the Son of God.'[14]"

He looked me straight in the eye. "I believe and I do have the Son of God."

"Also, do you subscribe to the following? 'If thou shalt confess with thy mouth the Lord Jesus, and shalt believe in thine heart that God hath raised him from the dead, thou shalt be saved.'[15]"

Again he affirmed his faith. "I do so confess."

I shared with him my own deep spiritual experiences in my personal times of bereavement and sorrow and told him how, through prayer and faith, I had received the divine assurance that somewhere, somehow, we would meet again. "You *are* a believer, aren't you?" he said. "And thank you, for you have strengthened my own faith. May I say to you that I, too, believe. I'm comforted. I, too, am sure." And he added, "I like a minister who believes, knows why he believes, and does not hesitate to witness to his belief."

Mr. Sloan has now himself moved on from this world to the other side, and that his faith and mine have been verified I have no doubt whatsoever.

LORD THOMSON'S QUESTION

Another rugged friend of mine was the late Lord Thomson of Fleet. Roy Thomson was one of the few great newspapermen of our era. At one time he owned and operated some 240 newspapers in England, Scotland, Canada, and the United States. He had a reputation for buying and selling newspapers, and his enjoyment of

14. 1 John 5:11–13   15. Romans 10:9

this business career was a byword throughout the English-speaking world. He was born the son of a country preacher in Canada; his father had very little of this world's goods, but he gave to his son a depth of faith that unmistakably showed when I knew him years later.

Roy Thomson forged ahead in the newspaper business, finally owning such famous papers as the *London Times*, the *Sunday Times of London* and the *Scotsman*, of Edinburgh. He was created, finally, a peer of the realm, Lord Thomson of Fleet.

One day he invited me to be guest of honor at a luncheon in the sumptuous dining room of the *London Times*. The company about the table was made up of the distinguished editors and writers of the *Sunday Times*, as well as prominent businessmen of the British capital. The table conversation ranged over many themes: world affairs, politics British and American, and the prospects for world peace. Suddenly, in the midst of general conversation, Lord Thomson said, "Dr. Peale, I would like to propound a question and I would appreciate a straightforward yes or no answer, if you don't mind. You see, I am becoming an old man, and one of these days I'm going to die." Silence sang in the room. "What I want to know is this: Is there an afterlife, do you believe in it, and if so, why? Tell me, for I really want to know."

Prior to this time there had been much humor and good-natured banter, but this took a serious tone. I wasn't really sure that he wasn't, shall I say, pulling my leg a bit. But then I sensed that the question was indeed on his mind, that he was really serious. All those present listened intently.

"Well, Lord Thomson," I said, "I am no great scholar,

only a preacher, but I am a committed Christian and believe in the promises written in the Holy Bible. I believe in immortality, in life after death, in the Christian plan of salvation for time and eternity. I am a believer, sir, and say to you that if you are in Christ you will be with Him in paradise." I stated to him the same Biblical truths as I had to Mr. Sloan.

"But even beyond the Biblical, my Lord, is the evidence of intelligence and common sense. You are a man of rational, intelligent mind and you appreciate that which makes sense."

Then I went on to tell him and the others a parable, and I noted the profound interest not only of his Lordship but of the entire luncheon company. The parable was about a baby in the prenatal state tucked up under his mother's loving heart. "Suppose," I said, "that someone might come to this unborn baby and say, 'You cannot stay here very long. In a few months you will be born, or, as you may think of it, die out of your present state.' The baby might stubbornly remonstrate, 'I don't want to leave here. I'm comfortable, well cared for; I'm warm, loved, and happy. I don't want to be what you call born or what I call die out of this place.'

"But in the normal course of events he is born. He does die out of his present life. And then what does he find? He feels beneath him strong, loving arms. He looks up into a beautiful face, tender with love, the face of his mother. Everyone runs to meet his pleasure. Everyone loves him. He is welcomed, cuddled, cared for. And he might say, 'How foolish I was. This is a wonderful place to which I have come. I'm so happy here.'

"Then he goes on to develop as a child and enjoys all the wondrous delights of childhood. He grows into youth with all of its excitement and romance. He marries, and his children play about him. He holds their little hands and knows their love. So the years pass, with the strength of manhood, the achievement of middle age; the joy and wonderment of life are his.

"Then he becomes an old man. His hair is white, his step slower; his natural energy abates. Someone might come to him and say, 'You cannot stay here. You are going to die, or, as we might call it, be born out of this place into another.' And he might remonstrate, 'But I don't want to die. I like it here. It is warm and pleasant and I have my loved ones. I love this world—dawning, and sunset, and the moon at night, and the starlight. I like to feel the warmth of the fire on my face when cold weather comes, and to hear the crunch of snow beneath my feet on a winter's night. I like springtime and summertime and falltime and wintertime. I love this world. I don't want to leave it, I don't want to die.'

"But there comes a time when in natural course he does die. What happens then? Is God, the Creator, suddenly going to change His nature? Can we not assume that he will feel once again loving arms beneath him, and once again look up into a strong, beautiful face, more lovely even than that first face he saw so long ago? Won't he soon be exclaiming, 'Why, this is wonderful! This place is surpassingly beautiful. I love this new life. Here I want to remain forever.'

"Does this not make sense?" I concluded, suddenly realizing that I had talked too long. A deep silence hung over the table. Men coughed. Some brushed tears from their eyes. Lord Thomson sighed. "It does indeed make sense," he said. "I will never forget that parable. It has helped me by answering questions that have haunted me for years."

Then suddenly his mood changed. "Do you think I will like it over there?" he asked.

"Of course you will, for it will be exciting, and you've always been an exciting man."

"What do you think I will do there?" he asked with a grin.

"Knowing you, I think you may perhaps buy and sell newspapers!" A laugh went around the table as the luncheon party broke up.

But on the way to the elevator Lord Thomson put his arm around my shoulder. "I have always thought of you as a teacher of positive thinking," he said. "You know something, my friend? You are also a man of God. And I like you for both!"

Since then Lord Thomson has gone on into the life beyond. I think God must be taking care of this lovable man, judging by the affirmative way he responded to the faith and the power.

7

How the Power
Came to Some

THE WEATHER WAS HOT THAT AUGUST SUNDAY. But in the large New Jersey church an enthusiastic capacity congregation seemed to have an awareness that the Spirit of the Lord was present in power. Such an atmosphere and spiritual climate is, of course, an important aid in the preaching of the gospel. Mary Brinig, one of Marble Collegiate's most effective members, once defined a church service as "the development of an atmosphere in which a spiritual miracle may take place." So I had the feeling on this occasion that lives were being changed by the work of the Holy Spirit; by the power. And so it proved.

Particularly to be remembered is one person present that day because her situation represents one important reason why many people never have a life-changing spiritual experience. They are unwilling to let go of resentment and hate. On this Sunday I was the guest preacher, and after the service, while greeting a long line of people, this woman came along. She was somewhat on the young side of middle age, well dressed and attractive, but made this surprising statement: "I always itch. I itch more than ever when I go to church. But today the itch was unbearable, more than ever before."

"Well, madam," I responded rather jocularly to this extraordinary statement, "I've had all sorts of results from my sermons, but this is the first time I've ever been held responsible for itching."

Ignoring this pleasantry, she said (and I became aware that she was very serious and not in any sense an oddball type), "I mean it, Dr. Peale, and I'm in great distress. I have read your books—all of them, I think— and when I saw in the newspaper that you were to preach here today I just had to come. Please help me." I asked her to step aside until I had spoken with the others, then turned again to her. "Just look at my arm," she said, "just see that itch." I looked at her arm but, aside from what might have been a mild redness, it seemed normal to me. The thought came that perhaps the "itching" might not be physical but perhaps mental or even spiritual in origin. I told her that I had to leave just then to keep another engagement, but if she wished to do so she might make an appointment through my secretary and I would see her in my office.

SHE HATED HER SISTER

In an interview a few days later she informed me that she almost constantly suffered from an itching sensation and, strangely enough, when she went to church it invariably increased in intensity. She had, however, never mentioned this curious fact to her minister, whom I knew to be a man of insight and wisdom. Then she repeated her statement that when I preached in the New Jersey church the sensation of itching was much more intense; indeed, almost unbearable. She added that for some time she had persistently run a degree of temperature and constantly felt as though a cold was coming on, though none ever seemed to develop.

I became interested in her case and began to probe for mental or spiritual trouble of which this itching problem might be an outer physical manifestation. As it developed, my guess proved accurate. I asked if she minded my talking with her physician and she agreed that I might do so. She was aware that I had founded the Institutes of Religion and Health and she had expressed an interest in going to that clinic for help.

The doctor was a cooperative man and, indeed, spoke favorably of our work in the field of mental health, saying that in his opinion the pastor and the doctor were natural allies in helping people to live healthy lives. He stated that according to his findings there was nothing physically or organically amiss with this patient, but made the provocative statement that she had developed a neurosis or obsession that might be described as a kind of "inner mental eczema, a scratching on the inside that, to her, seemed to be on the skin." When I asked about the degree of temperature and the feeling as if a cold was coming on, he seemed to think that this also was a mild but uncomfortable physical manifestation of a disturbed mental state.

"Actually, Dr. Peale," he said, "the whole problem in this case may be more in your field than in mine. I happen to know that she and her only sister have been on the outs, and it just might be that some aspect of her problem may be found in that area." I told him that when I had tried to probe into her spiritual life she shied off. "She's pretty introverted," he observed.

In a second interview, armed with the foregoing background, I said to the woman, "Your doctor and I— he a physician of the body and I also a doctor, a physician of the soul—have had a scientific consultation about you, our patient, and together we have come to the conclusion that yours is perhaps a soul sickness. So tell me, what is this about your sister? I advise you to bring this matter out if you want relief and well-being."

Startled, she flushed and was obviously embarrassed. "I . . . I . . . I'm a Christian woman, Dr. Peale. I've been saved from sin. I'm a faithful church member."

"Yes," I encouraged her, "I know that you are a sincere Christian and a good woman and a saved person. But, as of course you know, the Devil or Satan is always on the job. And he gets his deviltry in, not only in connection with what we call the gross sins, but with the more subtle sins, like those of the disposition. He makes us think that these are higher-class attitudes that are really not evil, and then he twists our minds so that we get to telling ourselves that since we are not guilty of the grosser sins, we are perfectly justified in resenting, even hating, someone who we think has wronged us. And then we find that the personality cannot get along with a rationalized evil in the system and so we begin to suffer thereby."

She sat silent as I continued. "So sometimes we have to perform an operation and remove the bad foreign body that is causing suppuration, or the sending off of a kind of pus through the entire system. One of the worst of these is hate. It is very violent in its reaction, especially when it becomes lodged in a good person." I then quoted to her those cleansing words from the fifteenth chapter of John, verse three: "Now ye are clean through the word which I have spoken unto you." "We are going to make you clean," I told her, "through the Word, the powerful, positive faith of Jesus Christ, your Savior, and the way to begin the process is simply for you to tell me all about it."

She smiled a weak, sad smile. "We don't really know, sometimes, why we do things. But I guess, Dr. Peale, that I came to you because I knew you would understand; you are a kind man and a true believer. Oh, help me to find peace again!" The story she told was not a complex one, simply a difference of opinion between two loving sisters over the disposition of the proceeds from their deceased father's estate. They were the only heirs, their mother having died some years earlier. The other sister had a family of two children, while this sister was unmarried. The father had tried to take this extra need into account in parceling out their inheritance. But one thing had led to another; they couldn't get together on the matter. Suspicion flared and grew into charges of double-crossing. And since a human being can hate more violently one who was previously loved, the gulf between the two widened. This sister would no longer speak to the other. Her hatred became vitriolic. And being of a sensitive and highly organized nature, her personality could not accommodate the hate, especially since it activated an enormous sense of guilt, and apparently tried to throw it out by means of the itching.

THE CURATIVE WAS LOVE

"Do you love Jesus?" I asked. She nodded.

"Was He ever mistreated?"

"Yes."

"Did He hate anyone?"

"No. But I'm not Jesus."

"No, but remember what he said: 'He that believeth on me, the works that I do shall he do also; and greater works than these shall he do.'[1] That means that you can overcome this hate."

"I'm a sinner," she said.

"That's a good start," I commented. "Now tell God that you are sorry for this sin and ask Him to take the hate away." She did as directed, but very slowly, though sincerely. "Now comes the big hurdle," I said, "but you are a big soul with a big faith in Christ. Now you must say, 'I love my sister. I forgive her if she has wronged me.'" Then, to my surprise, she blurted out,

1. John 14:12

"She didn't wrong me. I built it all up in my mind. She is the sweetest person on earth. I'm a fool."

I watched the struggle taking place in the woman. Hate and love are ambivalent reactions, and sometimes people enjoy hating even though they hate the pain it causes—not unlike the sadistic pleasure in biting down on a sore tooth. She wanted to let the hate go, yet did not want to part with it. She had lived with it for four years until it had come to dominate her mind. "What wonderful relief it will be," I said, "when you let that hate go. The itching will go with it and your temperature will drop to normal." So I went all-out in promise.

"Dear Jesus," she said, head bowed, "with Your help I now let my hate go. Take it all, Lord, and forgive me by Your grace."

"What is your sister's telephone number?" I asked. I dialed the number she gave me.

"Oh, I can't, I can't!" she exclaimed.

"Oh, yes, you can and you must." The sister answered the telephone. "This is Norman Vincent Peale," I said. "Your sister wants to speak to you." My patient took the phone. There was a long hesitation. "Oh, I do love you," she said, and burst into tears. I could hear similar weeping from the other end. Two sisters together crying out their disagreement and feeling love returning. Dabbing her eyes, the woman made signs of apology to me. "Keep it going," I said. "Good, healthy crying is great therapy. It washes out the soul."

At her specific request I did not tell her pastor of this healing, but on meeting her doctor by chance on the street, he said to me, "That's pretty good medicine of yours!"

"He *is* quite a Physician, isn't He?" I said.

"Sure is—He sure is," he replied. Thus ended one of my interesting case history demonstrations of the positive power of Jesus Christ. Final report: no more itching, temperature normal.

HAROLD WANTED POWER IN HIS LIFE

He was a big, rather tough-looking man with a demure-appearing wife, but as I later learned, she was no softy. They started attending services regularly at Marble Collegiate Church and so presently came to my attention, especially since, as he put it, he "finagled" a seat near the front.

One Sunday after the service he and Freda found their way back to my office, overawed my usually resolute secretary, and were ushered into my study. "Doctor," he said, "I first heard you at the national convention of our textile industry and you clicked with me. I was brought up in a churchgoing family down south, but then Freda and I drifted away. After hearing you speak at the convention we decided—that is, Freda did—that we would come to your church every Sunday. You are always talking about this spiritual power business, getting on top of tension and worry and all that stuff. And that's what I want. But somehow, even though I try to follow your ideas, I don't quite get the hang of it. Do you think if I started reading the Bible I would get onto it?" So ran his blunt but obviously sincere remarks.

I found myself liking this man. Freda, who stood by, said, "Don't let him fool you, Dr. Peale. He isn't as tough as he would have you believe. He is a big, soft-hearted, lovable, overgrown kid. But you have reached him with the gospel and he is looking to find the Lord. And when the Lord gets him, believe me, He will have somebody."

"Aw, don't pay any attention to her," he said, but the look he gave her showed a bond between these two that touched me.

I took a sheet of paper and wrote, "Matthew, Mark, Luke, John," and handed it to him saying, "Read those four books in the Bible and pray as you read. Concentrate on those four, no more now, and I believe the power of the Lord will start working in you." Harold stuck the paper in his pocket. "Come on, honey," he said to his wife, "let's get busy on lesson number one." With a wave of the hand he went out, followed by the not so demure Freda.

Some time went by and the couple was there in that down-in-front pew every Sunday. Then I had a phone call from Harold. "Hey, Norman, you and Ruth want a good dinner? I know how busy you are, but when you get a free night how about coming over? I know she doesn't look like it, but that gal Freda can really cook— good old southern cooking."

"Sure, Harold, we would love to do that," I replied, and we settled upon a night. The dinner lived up to the enthusiastic advance billing, and the visit was the unalloyed pleasure one has with real, down-to-earth folk.

After dinner Harold got down to business, spiritual business. He said, "I'm trying, really trying. I hear you talking about finding Christ and what a terrific experience that is and the joy and peace and power that goes with it, but still I don't get it and I really want to, I really do; furthermore, I mean to find it. Now, look." He walked over and picked up a Bible from a table. "Look at that Bible. After talking with you I went out and bought it. Best quality leather, gold edges, and it's protected by a zipper around three sides. Set me back fifty bucks. And I have read Matthew, Mark, Luke, and John all the way through six times, and I've prayed, too, like you said."

THE MISSING INGREDIENT

Realizing there was some missing ingredient, we had a wide and discursive conversation about Harold's life, both personally and in business. In the discussion I began to notice some uncomplimentary remarks about a Jewish business competitor named Finkelstein. The more this man's name came up in our conversation, the more I realized that Harold literally detested him. At first I feared it might represent an anti-Semitic attitude, but soon abandoned that notion. His antipathy was based entirely on Mr. Finkelstein's business acumen and ability, but to Harold he was a "no-account, dirty, lying, double-crossing crook." Freda insisted he was no such thing, just too smart for Harold. But her husband gave his competitor no credit at all, simply "hating his guts," as he rather inelegantly put it.

It did not require a great deal of insight to isolate the problem that was frustrating this sincere man in his spiritual search. "There is no way out of it, Harold. You will just have to learn to love Finkelstein if you want spiritual power."

"Love that unprincipled, double-crossing skunk? That's out, and I mean *out!*"

"In that case, you yourself are out, for love is the one way." I read to him the thirteenth chapter of First Corinthians and pointed out that "love never faileth." We reviewed the story of the good Samaritan, called his attention to the love that flowed from the Cross of Calvary, and emphasized that love is the center of Christ's message. "You will just have to love Finkelstein, old boy, and tonight when you go to bed I want you to pray for Mr. Finkelstein that he will have good success in his business." He leaped from his chair. "Me pray for that old buzzard and his business? Why, he has already stolen from me all that he knows!"

But the next day he telephoned. "O.K., you win. I got down on my knees and prayed for that guy. I told the Lord I was doing so only because you insisted on it. But then I told Him I would try to mean it. I kept on praying and finally discovered that I did mean it."

"You're real, Harold, you are real, 100 percent real. In my opinion the Lord just can't help liking you."

Harold's spiritual change did not happen overnight, but one Sunday I noticed a couple sitting with him and Freda in the church pew. I did not recognize these other people, but had a hint as to their identity when Harold looked up at me in the pulpit and nodded his head toward the man accompanying him. Later the four of them came into my study. "This is an old buzzard named Finkelstein," said Harold, "one of the best businessmen in New York."

"Forget it," said Mr. Finkelstein. "This old coot runs rings around me."

"Freda," I exclaimed in astonishment, "these two fellows actually seem to love each other!" When ill will broke down and dissolved, Harold found the power he had been seeking. He demonstrated that when one finds the block between himself and Christ and surrenders it, he is rewarded in full measure. Then the power comes through.

HE GAVE HIMSELF TOTALLY TO CHRIST

To some the power comes through victory over resentment, hate, and ill will; to some by relentless seeking; to still others by a sudden and total giving of self to Christ the Savior. In my long experience in the ministry I have had a part in the spiritual pilgrimage of many in all such categories. Recalling these wonderful persons, there comes to mind the memory of my dear friend Paul Soupiset. My first contact with Paul was via radio. After his wife and children left home for Sunday school and church, he was in the habit of listening to my talks in his home in Houston, Texas. He told me later that he listened sleepily, as he was generally recovering from a Saturday night party.

On this particular Sunday morning the radio message had to do with the emptiness of life which so often plagues people who are unconsciously reaching for something meaningful. Paul listened as we told what life with Christ could mean in terms of peace, joy, excitement. He was deeply dissatisfied with his life, and when finally I suggested over the air that any listener could have a new and wonderful life through commitment to Christ, he got out of bed, went down on his knees and then and there, under the influence of the radio message, gave his life in its totality to Jesus Christ. As spectacular as it may seem, he immediately became a changed man. His life took on increased dimensions, a deeper meaning. He now had a purpose instead of his previous aimlessness.

Shortly thereafter, Paul, who was in the ladies' ready-to-wear business, was transferred to a shop in San Antonio, Texas. Spurred on by his new and vital spiritual experience, he looked about in his new location for an opportunity to serve the Lord in a creative and vital manner.

LITTLE CHURCH OF LA VILLITA

He discovered a little church building, long in disuse, standing in the heart of the area known as La Villita, the center out of which the present city of San Antonio developed. He persuaded those who owned the church property to permit him, as a lay preacher, to conduct Sunday evening evangelistic services. Soon the little church was crowded by a congregation consisting of all sorts of people of every color, denomination, and nationality gathered together for the common purpose of finding the Lord Jesus and establishing a vital relationship with Him.

Paul always seemed to entertain a strong feeling of gratitude toward me for being what he called "the agent of my conversion." So when he was ready to install a set of carillon bells in the church tower he invited me to come and dedicate them in a special service. He even said the bells were to be dedicated to me, and since I was touched by his enthusiastic discipleship and had never had any bells dedicated to me before, I accepted his invitation to speak on the proposed occasion.

The little church was crowded to capacity that night and Paul was in his glory, welcoming his "congregation" and telling them in his own winsome way about Jesus, who, he said, was present there with all of us. Then he introduced one of his most active workers who, he confided to me, was a former drunk. This man would perform the act of dedicating the bells. That this big, burly fellow was not used to public speaking was quite evident by the embarrassed manner in which he functioned. But his sincerity was equally evident. Coming to the podium, he said something like the following: "Friends and fellow citizens, we hereby dedicate these bells to the glory of God and in memory of Norman Vincent Peale." Everyone roared, and in the midst of the laughter I pointed out that I was not dead quite yet. In any event it was a happy and joyous gathering.

Following my sermon, which was, of course, an evangelistic witness, Paul gave the invitation to all who desired to find new life in Christ to come and kneel at the altar. Some forty people crowded the altar asking God for forgiveness and salvation. Paul went along speaking to each one in his own loving manner. One was a Mexican man. "*Amigo*, you want Christ?" asked Paul.

"*Si, Senor* Paul, *si, Senor*," he replied with great sincerity. A little girl knelt there, head bowed. "Do you love Jesus, honey?" Paul asked.

"Oh, yes, I do, Mr. Soupiset," she murmured. A very well-dressed elderly lady, white-haired and dignified, looked up with clasped hands. "And you, too, want to find Him?"

"Oh, yes, sir, I want peace in my heart and forgiveness for my sinful life." Paul looked down upon her with compassion. Then, to my surprise, he placed both of his hands upon her head. "Receive Jesus," he said. Tears flowed from her eyes, and from mine also. Through this erstwhile "sinner" the positive power of Jesus Christ was being transmitted before my very eyes to the people, rich and poor, black and white, young and old, Mexican and American. It was all so very wonderful.

As I walked out of the little church of La Villita that evening into the old historic city of San Antonio, the bells in the tower sang into the night air those words of grace: "I love to tell the story . . . of Jesus and His love." I thanked God that He had given me the great privilege of winning to Christ this wonderful man, Paul Soupiset, who himself was bringing into the Lord's Kingdom so many of His lost children.

On another occasion Paul was honored at a huge open-air meeting in San Antonio to which I was invited, and again I witnessed the remarkable power of this redeemed man to persuade people of all sorts that Jesus alone has the answer. I shall never forget that night when thousands gathered to pay him tribute, including the mayor and other distinguished citizens. He was assuredly one of those great human beings to whom the power came in full measure.

TOP MIDSHIPMAN

An amazing fact about the positive power of Jesus Christ is that it moves across the entire gamut of life, touching and changing and vitally affecting persons of all types, all strata of economic standing, all levels of education, every sort and condition of mankind. In fact, it may be appropriately termed the one great, all-embracing, universal factor in the life of mankind.

A newspaper staff writer, Bruce Friedland, tells of Naval Academy honor graduate Arthur Athens. Following is the newspaper article describing the event:

Besides being the brigade commander in charge of all the midshipmen, Athens is among the 99 honor graduates who excelled academically.

His 3.6 average on a scale of 4.0 earns him the special recognition of being handed his diploma by President Jimmy Carter, a former midshipman himself, who will address the 956 graduating seniors Wednesday. Athens could easily be an advertisement for the academy with his clean-cut appearance, articulate speech, and general self-discipline. More discipline, most likely, than most of his peers.

"I have always been fairly disciplined all my life . . . self-disciplined," he says. That's the reason he chose a service school instead of a regular university. The "leadership opportunities" are better in the military, he explains.

There are ties to the military that Athens feels strongly about. He is prepared to fight for his country. When asked about that possibility, he tenses slightly, reminding himself of the commitment.

"I am deeply religious," he says, and there are tough questions to answer about religious people taking lives. "But it's better to have God-fearing people in the military" than those who have no morals, he explains.

Brigade Commander Arthur Athens received his diploma and commission papers from President Carter and W. Graham Clayton, Secretary of the Navy, at commencement exercises at the U.S. Naval Academy in Annapolis.

Lieutenant Athens wrote the following letter to me, pointing out the positive power of Jesus Christ in his life and career:

Dear Dr. Peale,

I just graduated two weeks ago from the United States Naval Academy. I have been receiving sermons and inspirational material from you since my early days in high school.

I can honestly say that it was you, Dr. Peale, and God's inspiration that allowed me to draw close to Jesus Christ, and recognize Him as friend and Savior. A day hasn't passed where I haven't been reading your latest sermon, books that you have written, or pamphlets that you've developed for positive living.

The Academy is a very, very difficult four-year program of academics, training, and discipline. There certainly have been many discouraging times, but through faith, confidence, and enthusiasm we have overcome these challenges. From a lowly plebe in my first year at the Academy I have reached the peak of God's success at Annapolis. I graduated as an honor graduate, the Brigade Commander (in charge of 4,300 midshipmen), and the recipient of the alumni award given to top midshipman of the graduating class in the areas of academics, athletics, and leadership combined. I can state these honors with all humbleness and with a thankful heart for God's goodness and your inspiration.

The alumni award consisted of a $1000 check, and I want to present one-tenth of that gift to the Foundation for Christian Living, specifically to assist in the building of the $750,000 expansion of the Foundation for Christian Living headquarters in Pawling, New York.

I look forward to starting a career in the United States Marine Corps armed with hundreds of your pamphlets and books. That inspirational material will make the difference with God's help.

Thank you for all you have done for me, and I continue to pray for you, Dr. Peale.

Sincerely,
Lt. Arthur J. Athens

So the power came to a brilliant student, an honor graduate of the United States Naval Academy.

A WALL STREET BANKER AND THE POWER

He was both a banker and a scholar, and he was my next door neighbor when I lived at 40 Fifth Avenue, New York City. We had many a talk about life and philosophy and religion. His major interest was in the latter, for in his opinion the two greatest minds ever to appear in history were those of Jesus and Paul, and he made an attempt to condition his mind to theirs. He was an international banker and had to do with many of the most complex financial matters relevant to our time.

He read the Bible daily in three languages—English, French, and Spanish—and claimed to find differing and enlightening nuances in the Holy Scriptures in these three language forms. So important was this Bible reading to him in his daily personal and work schedule that he made it a practice to arrive at his Wall Street office each day well before seven o'clock so that he could "condition my mind spiritually" before the office work day began at nine o'clock.

He believed that this practice of Bible reading put his mind in such a state that his mental processes were open to insights, intuitions, and understandings that would not be possible otherwise. He believed that Christ could not only "save" him on the moral and spiritual level but in the mental area also, by making him sensitively aware of truth and rightness to such an extent that he could actually do no wrong but inevitably function on the law of God. He was a man of impeccable character and beauty of spirit.

He told me that once he had a "terribly important" negotiation in Boston to which he went by train that he might have adequate time to "condition my mind and

spirit that I might be in an attitude of maximum understanding and, beyond that, sympathetic feeling for the
others involved." To bring himself to this state of mind
and spirit, he read St. Paul for an hour, for, said he,
"Paul had one of the few most acute minds ever to appear on this earth." This, he said, tended to make his
own mind keen and sharp and also to keep him spiritually and intellectually sensitive to the feelings and rights
of others. To this remarkable and deeply dedicated
Christian man the positive power of Jesus Christ meant
not only salvation from immorality and sin, but also a
sensitive refinement of personality, an in-depth feeling
for people, and a mental appreciation of all that is good
and true.

A LITTLE GIRL SEES THE POWER WORK
Even as the power was demonstrated in the life of a
brilliant and scholarly business leader, so it operated in
the experience of a little girl. She had a simple belief in
prayer, and of course the Lord heard and answered her
prayers, and ours, too, for we joined her in spiritual
fellowship.

Susan's letter really touched my heart. It reads as follows:

> Dear Dr. Norman Vincent Peal;
>
> I have this problem that I would like you to send me some booklets on. My mother is on dope and I am living with my Grandmother. My mother never married We don't get to see her very often. That's my sister and I. And could you put her on your pray list. I go to church every Sunday I am only 9 years old so I don't really understand.
>
> Yours truly
> Susan

My associates at the Foundation for Christian Living joined me in earnest and continuous prayer as Susan had requested. Then, nearly three years later, a second letter, this one typewritten, came from Susan and it was full of happiness. She had seen the positive power of Jesus Christ at work. She says:

Dear Dr. Peale

I don't know if you remember me or not. I wrote you a letter when I was nine I told you about my Mother and the problems I was having understanding all of it. I am 12 now and I'm in the 7th grade. Today I am a happier girl than I was then. My mother is all so much better. She came to see us (my sister and I) she surprised me so much she was completely changed and she wasn't on dope or anything and hadn't been. I have an aunt and she had helped her a lot but nothing helped her like all the prayers that were siad for her that is what my letter is mainly for I want to thank you for your prayer that was said for her and I can fell asuared that it was heard. I have joined the Church and that is one thing that makes me happier. My Grandmother is well and still working hard mabye harder than she was the last time I wrote. Your litature has meant alot to me and my Grandmother Let me end this letter with my thanks to you again.

Yours truly,
Susan

AT THE SHEPHERDS' FIELDS

I have always marveled at the constant way in which Jesus Christ is ever present and at work in the lives of people. Every day, every night, everywhere, in every circumstance, the Lord is among us and His gracious helpfulness goes on constantly and continuously. He is never very far from anyone of us; indeed, "Closer is He than breathing, and nearer than hands and feet."[2] That He loves every one of us, especially those who name His name as Lord and Savior, there can be no doubt at all. In every moment of need He is nearby to help us. This fact has to be one of the few greatest comforts in this world.

Bob came to church one day and he was frightened. On Monday he was scheduled to enter a hospital for tests, and he had come to feel that something was very wrong with him. As he sat in the church that Sunday morning, fear, dark and sinister, lurked in his mind. He desperately wanted help; he needed to feel peace and assurance.

Bob was a former Air Force captain and a man of

2. From "The Higher Pantheism," st. 6, by Alfred, Lord Tennyson

faith, though not necessarily of deep personal commitment. As he sat in his pew with his wife he prayed earnestly, and a strange feeling came that he was being watched over and protected; he even felt that something great was about to happen to him. And indeed it did.

I ended my sermon that day by stating that I was going directly from the pulpit to an adjoining room and that anyone who personally felt the need for prayer and who desired a closer relationship with Christ was invited to meet me there. To my surprise, the room, which could accommodate perhaps 200 persons, was completely filled. We had a deep and meaningful prayer session in which we prayed for all those present who requested it.

Bob, who was sitting in the front seat, got up and said, "Dr. Peale, I am in deep distress and I need the prayers of all the good people here. I am facing I don't know what tomorrow at the hospital. I need courage and strength and faith." I moved over to his side and put my hand on his shoulder. I could actually feel him shaking all down through his body. I prayed for him, asking the people to join in earnest petition to God for this deeply disturbed man. When we said, "Amen" I happened to look straight at him and was astounded and deeply moved by the expression that passed over his face. It was a kind of mixture of wonderment, peace, and joy, although tears stood in his eyes. I put my hand again on his shoulder and could detect no sign of the shaking that had been present earlier.

He came through his physical problem successfully and thereafter was a regular and dedicated worshiper at the church. When Mrs. Peale and I announced that we intended to take a party to the Holy Land and visit the places where Jesus walked, Bob and his wife joined the tour party. One day we were at the Shepherds' Cave, the roof of which is blackened by centuries of fires. It is said that this cave had been used by shepherds for shelter during cold nights over long centuries. The fields nearby are called the Shepherds' Fields. From the site of the cave, Bethlehem can be clearly seen, situated as it is upon elevated ground on a hilltop. Presumably this could be the spot where the shepherds saw the heavens open and where the star came to rest. Perhaps it was here that they said, "Let us now go even unto Bethlehem, and see this thing which is come to pass, which the Lord hath made known unto us."[3]

Bob stood looking toward Bethlehem, and I noted that he was profoundly and emotionally stirred. Tears were on his cheeks. Pointing in the direction of Bethlehem, he said in a choked voice, "Whatever would have happened to me had He not been born over there?" And I added, "He was born twice for you—once in Bethlehem and again that day in Marble Collegiate Church."

So the power came to another man, though through different circumstances. The coming of the power is so great that it enters people's lives according to their needs and their types of personality. The power follows no set or routine procedure, the only absolute being a letting go of self through commitment to Jesus Christ as Lord and Savior. We are saved by faith, however and whatever the method by which the saving comes. In every case it is the positive power of Jesus Christ in operation.

3. Luke 2:15

WHEN FAITH BECOMES POSITIVE

When we couple the term "positive" with the name of Jesus, we do so in humble reverence. The name of Jesus is sacred beyond all names. The faith He taught was a positive faith based on belief in the Word, belief in the Holy Spirit, belief in God. And belief of that quality releases the power in human life. It washes away sin, fear, doubt, and every form of blockage to the redeemed life of joyful freedom.

The gospel of Christ teaches us to be aware of all human suffering and of the evil in the world; of all satanic power. But it also teaches that "this is the victory that overcometh the world."[4] Positive thinking is no blithe and superficial Pollyanna type of thought. It sees all the difficulty and pain of human existence; nor is it abashed and defeated by what it sees, for it knows that, by the power of God in Christ, the believer enters into that victory which does indeed overcome the world.

Perhaps the writer of the following letter had the experience of release from negativism to the positive power through a deeper faith. He is the head of a firm of management consultants in a large southern city:

> Dear Dr. Peale,
>
> I became a believer in Jesus Christ almost 20 years ago. At that time my pastor was a very negative individual who was much opposed to concepts of positive thinking. My own outlook as a consequence was negative for many of those 20 years.
>
> As recently as three years ago as a result of this negative thinking, my personal world began to fall apart and my business life was beginning to suffer. Everything was frankly coming unglued, and then I received a copy of *Guideposts* and later the Foundation for Christian Liv-

4. I John 5:4

ing booklets. My own thinking began to turn around, and in the process the concept of Proverbs—that as a man thinks in his heart that is what he becomes[5] —began to get hold of my thinking.

I can only say that the Scripture, along with the materials I have been reading from you and your recent gift, *The Power of Positive Thinking*, have begun to revolutionize my life and the lives of my family. I am just sorry that I could not have had this power concept in my life years ago.

Because He lives,
Donald T. Redman

This letter indicates the new spirit of dedication to Christ that came to a longtime Christian when he had an experience of the positive power of Jesus Christ. That same positive power can come to anyone who will give heed to the Scripture, "Ask, and it shall be given you; seek, and ye shall find; knock, and it shall be opened unto you."[6]

5. Proverbs 23:7, paraphrased   6. Matthew 7:7

8

The Joy and the Power

THE JOY AND THE POWER GO TOGETHER.
They are twins. You can hardly have the one without
the other. Having the power results in joy. When the
joy comes, the power gets even stronger. The joy will
bubble out of you, and since you well know whence
such joy comes, you naturally praise the Lord and bless
His holy Name. Like what happened to Sam, for example.

Let me tell you about Sam, an unforgettable character. He is in Heaven now and must be spreading the
same joy he had here on earth after he experienced, in
his own big, robust way, the positive power of Jesus
Christ. This man was certainly a problem, a quite mixed
up though likable young man. He listened to my radio
sermons, which brought him to the church, and he read
all of my books, but never seemed to get any answers.
Instead, he always had more questions and he haunted
me constantly. He had graduated from college *magna
cum laude*, was a Phi Beta Kappa, and prided himself on
being an intellectual. Almost everywhere I went Sam
seemed to turn up with more questions.

Finally I said, "Look, Sam, I don't seem to help you.
Why not visit other churches in New York? Listen to
other preachers. They are excellent speakers and wise
Christian leaders. Surely with one of them you will find
the answers you seek and the peace and power you
want but are not finding." He took me at my word and
was absent for several Sundays. Then, there he was
again, looking down from the south balcony. Barging
back to my office after the service, he remarked, "Those
pastors are, as you say, great preachers, but they don't
know any more than you do; so here I am, back where
I started from."

"Sam, because of what happened to me when Christ

took over my life, I know that if you stop talking so much, lay off the questions, start practicing faith, confess your sins, and accept Jesus Christ, you will get all the answers you need." The remark about confessing his sins seemed to rock him a bit, for suddenly he turned quiet and shortly walked out.

DRAMA AT A HAMBURGER STAND

But he bounded back. One afternoon I emerged from the church to enter my car for a drive of some hundred miles upstate to give a talk. Standing by the car was Sam, who asked where I was going and immediately invited himself to go along. "Tell you what," he said brightly, "I will outline my problems on the way up and you can talk on the way back."

"Nothing doing," I replied. "I know all about your problems already—at least, all you've told me. About those you cover up with intellectual speculations I'm not so sure. You've never come clean about your sins, which is probably where your basic problem lies. Anyway, I have to think about my talk on the way. That is why I wanted to go alone," probably saying this a bit more maliciously than I should.

"O.K.," he said, "I will keep still, and we can talk on the return trip." I was not at all convinced he could remain silent for that long a time, but actually he did quite well for once.

On the return trip we discussed Sam's problems at length. Along about midnight we stopped at an attractive-looking hamburger place. Perched on stools at the counter, we each ordered a big "quarter-pounder" and coffee. Sam had just bitten into his sandwich when suddenly he put it down and banged his fist on the counter with such force that he made the silverware and the dishes, and me also, jump. "I've got it," he shouted, "I've got it at last!" The other customers looked up, startled. "Got what?" I asked.

"Now I know why everything goes wrong in my life. I'm wrong myself, that's why!"

"Never knew there was such power in a hamburger," I commented. "You have never admitted that wrongness idea before."

Sam sat still and was quiet. "I'm ready now," he finally said in a low voice. "I'm ready to do what you said about those sins of mine, and there are plenty of them." There was no one near at the counter and he poured out his mind. When he stopped there was a sigh of relief. "That's it, all the lousy stuff, and boy, what a relief to get that mess off my chest!" I paid the bill and we went out into the parking lot. Standing by the car, Sam talked to the Lord out loud, asking forgiveness and wholeheartedly giving his life to Jesus Christ. He stopped praying and I sensed that he was crying. Then the joy came through and he began to praise God and thank Him. He expressed his newfound joy all the way back to the city and his thoughts were those of wonderment, delight, and excitement. Actually, a new man was riding with me through that moon-drenched night. And I must add that he retained the joy, for he had found the power and it transformed his entire existence.

When the seeker after the power stops covering up the dirt in his life with intellectualism and rationalizations, the power comes surging in, and with it the joy. All of this is what we mean by the phrase, "the positive power of Jesus Christ."

HE HELPED HER STAND UP TO THINGS

Persons who have the power and also have the joy are the kind of folk who stand up to life, meet it courageously, and gain a victory over it. Some of these Christians have had it pretty rough, but adversity, instead of weakening their faith, only serves to make it stronger and more glorious.

I recall a woman out West, publisher of two weekly country newspapers. She was real and down to earth, a kind of rollicking, happy soul, so patently honest and good that you liked her at once. My last contact with her was several years ago, but when I began listing the persons I have known who had the joy and the power, she came to mind among others. Christ was actually the strength of her life in a realistic and practical sense. She had the joy in full measure.

I was scheduled to speak in her area and she wrote me asking for an appointment. The following was her forthright way of introducing herself:

I'm forty-three, built with broad shoulders, strictly all beef. [That was true, when I saw her, but that wasn't what I remember about her.] I can and do carry a load. Even after working long hours without rest I still feel bubbling with energy and hope. I have bright, clear blue eyes. I don't need glasses, though I read or write constantly. I have no gray hair and I feel young.

I'm never sick simply because I cannot afford the time or the money. Both my mother and my grandmother were crippled for years with arthritis, especially in the hands. But the minute it hit me I simply stated to my hands that they would have to type whether it hurt them or not and I asked God to make it possible. After a while the pain left my hands and so did the stiffness.

She took charge of herself! She wasn't going to be ruled by crippled, arthritic hands. Instead, she ruled them. Then she continued:

> I hardly ever get a cold except when I am discouraged. My last illness was a day off when my sixth son was born one Monday night, but I was able to get the newspaper out on Thursday just the same. The beloved Lord Jesus gives me this power, this victory power, this ability to stand up to life. I draw on it by faith and I never fail to know the truth that always wins.

This woman's belief is that, through Christ's help, you can stand up to anything, even dominate it.

Because the Lord gives calm control over circumstances and conditions, we have the victory formula that wins. This woman's personality revealed an infectious joyousness. She was the kind of person a Christian is designed to be, not free from the difficulty of this world, but one who, through Christ, has the power to stand up to it, to rise above it, to get on top of it and remain there. And along with that rugged power comes the lilting, heart-deep joy of victory.

"HE KEEPS ME SINGING"

Some who have the greatest power and the deepest joy have found both of these qualities the hard way through pain and sorrow, and it impresses me anew that Christianity may actually be called "the victory faith." The power often comes through suffering, the joy through tears; but when both come, it is in the form of unbreakable strength and totally inexpressible joy.

Take the story, which I have told elsewhere,[1] of Luther Bridgers, a down-South preacher, singer, and hymn writer. I was at his home for breakfast, where we had a happy time of friendship. That morning he told of his tragic experience when, as a young pastor, he went to another city to participate in a series of religious meetings. One night late he was awakened by the incessant ringing of the telephone. Over the wire came the voice of a friend hesitantly telling him the almost incredible news that fire had swept through his home while his wife and two children were sleeping. Every effort was made to save them, but the flames were too far advanced, and the three members of his family perished in the fire that destroyed his home.

Stunned, Luther dropped the receiver and sat suffering cruel mental agony. It couldn't be true! It just could not be true! Anguished beyond expression, he paced the floor. Then he bolted from the room and out of the hotel into the early-morning emptiness of the streets. For a long time he roamed up and down, desperately fighting for self-control.

In his agonizing search for peace he came to the dark river which flowed wide and deep through the town. He regarded it with fascination. In its cool depths lay forgetfulness. It would require only a moment of struggle for his spirit to leave his body and be reunited with his wife and little children. Life was so utterly impossible now. Impossible! Impossible! The word hammered at his brain. It was impossible to go on. He must die now in that swift-moving stream.

But deep within his mind was a long-established faith and trust. It held him steady. The struggle was intense.

1. *The Positive Principle Today*

He dropped finally to his knees, and the tears that had not yet come from dry eyes now poured out in a flood. Along with the tears was a prayer in depth for understanding and strength to handle this tragedy with the power always granted to a true believer. The inner conflict was long and hard, but in due course he found his way to life reconstruction. Later he married again and raised a second family in whose home I had breakfasted that morning.

Completing his tragic story, Luther sat at the piano and played with sensitive interpretation some music of the great composers. Then finally he went into one of his own well-known songs. I shall always be moved by the memory of this strong man singing joyous words known to thousands:

> *Jesus, Jesus, Jesus,*
> *Sweetest name I know,*
> *Fills my ev'ry longing,*
> *Keeps me singing as I go.*[2]

Golden sunlight streamed into the room, spotlighting the face of the singer. As he sang, a canary in a cage above the piano also began to sing. Man and bird seemed in perfect attunement as together they poured forth praise to the Lord who gives overcoming power to human beings. And who knows? Perhaps to birds also.

Luther Bridgers has to be on any list of strong and happy Christians. The power and the joy so characteristic of this man came out of almost incredible pain and suffering. But always Jesus Christ is there with His

2. From "He Keeps Me Singing." © Copyright 1910. Renewal 1937 Broadman Press. All rights reserved. Used by permission.

strong arm to help those who love and trust Him. Such persons win tough battles and finally emerge victorious, though not without scars.

VICTORY OF SUSIE BEIDEL

Another who received the power and the joy from Christ is Susie Hyun Sook Beidel. This girl had it rough, but she, too, came through to victory.

Susie was born in Korea; as an infant she suffered infantile paralysis and had one leg amputated. When refugees were flocking into South Korea as the communists swept through the north, she couldn't keep up with her family and was left behind, lonely and forlorn. Three GI's saw the little crippled girl limping along the road, picked her up, and took her to Pusan. After long months and much suffering she arrived in the United States. Later she married a fine young man, and the couple have two children.

They became members of my church, and now, at forty years of age, Susie is getting her college degree and moving into a career. She wrote to us recently:

> Dear Dr. and Mrs. Peale,
>
> I simply cannot let another day slip by without sharing some wonderful news with you—as the result of one of your sermons which had a profound effect on my life.
>
> You preached on "Why Positive Thinkers Get Positive Results." You said they are not controlled by the three L's—lack, loss, and limitation. They react positively to life, instead of fretting and mourning over what they don't have or what they've lost. You cannot expect right thoughts without pumping out wrong thoughts. Put your cherished dream in your mind, offer it to God, and keep thinking and working toward it.

Praying, thinking, and working equals undefeatable results! "I can do ALL things through Christ Jesus who strengtheneth me!"[3]

That sermon awakened me from my gloomy, stale, angry thoughts and regrets over the lack of opportunities in my life. Instead of shifting the blame on others and circumstances, I followed your advice.

I enrolled in the College of Staten Island. Initially I was quite shaken, for my educational background was not solid—I had never stepped into a high school. I earned a GED High School Diploma and one year of college before the children came along. At any event, I put your sermon to work. Believe me, it was not an easy task at the age of 40 with a family and social obligations.

However, through the help of God, my family, and the faculty and staff of the college, I completed the term and was awarded the "parchment" (B.A. in Psychology) *summa cum laude*. I can do ALL things through Christ Jesus who strengtheneth me!

I am deeply grateful to the Lord, to both of you, and the ministerial staff, for having instilled Positive Thinking into me.

Sincerely yours in Jesus,
"Susie" Hyun Sook Beidel

P.S. Currently I am working on my Master's degree in rehabilitation counseling at the St. John's University.

Of course Susie will make further progress. It is difficult to think of anyone who had it less opportune, who had fewer possibilities, than Susie. She was a young, poverty-stricken girl in Korea, limping along a highway on only one leg—a lonely child in the tidal wave of refugees from the surging communist host. Her story is corroboration of the thesis that Jesus Christ can do just about anything with the person who truly believes. To

3. Philippians 4:13

such strong, believing people come the power and the joy.

All human beings have hard and dark days when they believe, "I just can't make it. I can't do it. I haven't got what it takes." But this is not a valid appraisal to those who live with Him in totality of commitment. To them He gives the power and the victory and so the joy, always and inevitably.

A BUSINESSMAN'S JOY AND POWER

The joy and the power come to different persons in a variety of ways, according to God's providence and His will for the individual. One way is to practice the Jesus procedure in all matters. People using this method believe that always, whatever the problem, Jesus Christ has the answer, fully and completely.

This was true in the experience of Phillip, whom I first met in San Francisco on a speaking engagement. He had been reading my books and sermons for some time. I was at once struck by the happiness and obvious goodness of this man. Christ's spirit came through in him in a normal and natural fashion and his dedication was clearly apparent. Later Phillip and his wife, Eleanor, moved to New York City where he became a deacon in our church. He served in this capacity graciously, intelligently, and faithfully. Both of these people were earnestly desirous of growing in the Christian life. They sought to be believers in full stature and constantly applied their faith in whatever problems came to them. Phillip, who was the head of an important business, frequently consulted me, his pastor, about the application of Christian principles to business, particularly with reference to his employees. He seemed to feel that not only were their economic needs in his hands as president of the company, but, in a sense, their spiritual needs as well.

Once he telephoned late at night. Apologizing for the hour, he said that one of his associates was so much on his mind that he wondered if he might come over to talk and pray about the matter. He lived only a block up the street and of course I told him to come right along. The problem concerned the treasurer of his company, a good man, he explained, but a bit difficult to get along with.

The business was financial in nature and while Phillip himself was well-informed, he had come up on the administrative side of the company. He admitted that his treasurer was a financial genius. "He has forgotten more than I will ever know," said Phillip humbly. "But I have a leadership problem, for this man is openly contemptuous of me and is constantly criticizing and downgrading my ability and knowledge, asserting that he should be the president of our company, not I. And I'll have to admit that, from a strictly financial and technical point of view, he may be right. But what he does not seem to realize is that the company president's job is also to deal with people. In that department, I am sorry to say, he is woefully lacking, being very insensitive, even abrasive."

He reminded me that on his desk was a little framed sign which he had first seen in my office asking the question, "What would Jesus do?" It had so impressed him that he had one made for his own office. "What I want to do about Jim is what Jesus would do," he said simply. "And I've come to ask what you feel is the Jesus way in this situation."

So a businessman and a preacher talked far into the

night about the practical way to apply Christianity to a
personal and a business problem. I encouraged Phillip
to come up with his own ideas. "First thing is patience,
I guess, and then forbearance, not getting angry and
resentful," he said. "I want to think of Jim always as the
well-qualified and extremely capable man that he really
is." Both Phillip and I were close friends of the great
psychiatrist Dr. Smiley Blanton, and Phillip reminded
me that the doctor had always said, "When dealing
with a difficult person, always employ the scientifically
dispassionate method."

This means to ask thoughtfully, "Now, just why does
this individual react in such an unpleasant manner?
What is the personality problem behind these reactions?
What is eating at him?" Dr. Blanton also advised,
"Never react in kind; never become angry and flare up;
always consider the other person dispassionately, that
is, without passion or heat, and certainly with no strik-
ing back." Phillip meticulously went over the other
man's relationships and life style, trying to ascertain, if
possible, any clue to his personality problem. If he
could discover this, he would hope to do something
creative about it. As I recall, Phillip finally decided that
the man had a sense of insecurity despite his recognized
ability, and that this had developed a tension which
caused his irascibility.

Phillip suggested that we pray for Jim, asking for
guidance. I prayed first, asking insight for Phillip and
praying that the Lord might condition the associate to a
more controlled state of mind. When Phillip prayed it
was an outpouring of love and esteem for his treasurer,
humbly asking to be led to the right procedure in dealing with him. He prayed for wisdom in using the trea-

surer's outstanding ability and for insight on how to establish a good relationship between the other man and himself.

Wisdom and sensitivity resulted from that prayer conference. While fully exercising his function as president, Phillip let Jim become aware of the respect he had for his ability. Skillfully he built up the man's self-esteem and strengthened his sense of security. Phillip gradually gave the other man a wider scope in the operation of the business, and Jim began to see that Phillip not only respected but actually loved him as a person. As a result Jim gradually became more tractable, he began to take a personal interest in people, and, best of all, he learned to treat employees with greater considertion. When finally Phillip gave up the presidency to become chairman of the board, he made Jim president of the company. Months later I met Jim. "You know something?" he said. "Phillip is one of the best business leaders I've ever known. He is a very wise man. And," he added, "you and I know what a real Christian he is. He is my best friend."

One night Ruth and I were at the home of Phillip and Eleanor for dinner. When the guests were all seated in the dining room Phillip said, "Norman, I'm not going to ask you to offer the blessing, I'm going to do it myself. Let's all join hands. Dear Lord," he prayed, "thanks for making us all so happy, for taking such good care of us and for always guiding us. All of us love You very much. Amen."

As I looked at that happy man at the head of the table, his face relaxed and wreathed in smiles, I realized that he really had the joy and the power, the positive power of Jesus Christ.

A VIGOROUS DISCIPLE

He was a no-fooling sort of person. Anything could be accomplished if you had faith enough; so he believed. Indeed, this was the principle that motivated Fred R., one of the most enthusiastic and vigorous Christians of my experience. When he was changed by a Christian conversion he *really* changed.

But before his change he was a kind of wandering son of a good church family; not all that bad, perhaps, but neither was he in the kingdom of righteousness. He attended my church in New York occasionally, although he lived in Connecticut. I was not personally acquainted with him at the time. It seems that he was somewhat of a scoffer and had a particular dislike for the pastor of his church at home—called him a "stuffed shirt" and various other uncomplimentary designations.

One afternoon a friend telephoned him. "Hey, Fred, what are you doing tonight?" Fred fell into what turned out to be the Lord's trap. "Nothing. What's up?"

"The famous missionary Dr. E. Stanley Jones is preaching at a big meeting tonight in Hartford. Some of us are going. This man is one of the world's great preachers. Come along with us, since you have nothing scheduled."

"Are you kidding?" stormed Fred. "Me—go to hear a missionary? Come off it! Count me out. Nothing doing."

"Now, look, Fred," said his friend, "I've done some things for you. You have nothing to do tonight. So humor me and come along." Fred, always genial, a good fellow ever desiring to oblige, capitulated. "Oh, O.K., if you can stand it, guess I can, too. I'll go with you."

So Fred went to Hartford and sat in the seat of the

scornful. But not for long. Soon he sat upright from his slumped position, then leaned forward. Jones was getting to him—or was it the Christ, whom Jones represented so well, who was getting to him? With irrefutable logic and undeniable persuasion the great missionary put forward the claims of Christ that had won so many thousands during his epoch-making ministry in India.

Fred was enthralled, captivated, convinced. And when Dr. Jones announced that he was about to dismiss the huge crowd and invite those who were ready to accept Christ to remain, Fred said to the others, "I'm sticking around. This guy Jones is terrific." The others also stayed, and in that after-meeting Fred made the decision, as he put it, "to go the rest of the way with Jesus Christ."

When Fred was convinced, he was really convinced. When he was sold, he was really sold. Now that he was converted he wanted to "get going." When the group got back to their Connecticut town, even though it was after one o'clock in the morning, Fred insisted on going to the minister's house. He pounded on the door. "Hey, Reverend, wake up!" he cried. The tousled head of the minister appeared at the window. "What's going on down there? Who wants me, and what about?"

"It's Fred R.," said our spiritually reborn friend. "I've just been converted and you are the first person I want to see."

"Well," said the startled pastor, "O.K., but why couldn't you be converted at a more convenient hour? Hold on and I'll come down."

Soon Fred was excitedly telling the minister about the events of the evening; how he had gone to the meeting in Hartford, heard Stanley Jones, and accepted Christ, and now his life was changed. "And since I've never liked you and have said all kinds of mean things about you, I wanted you to be the first one I saw after my conversion, to tell you that I've been wrong about you. I want to tell you that now I love you and want to help you in the church in any way you want me to serve." The minister naturally was dumbfounded by the change in this young man, about whom he had an opinion that could not be considered the most favorable. But he responded in kind to the honest, enthusiastic outgoingness of the new convert and joined him in a prayer of thanksgiving for the great change which had come about in his life.

So they talked until night gave way to daybreak. "How about it if I rustle up some bacon and eggs, some toast and hot coffee?" said the pastor.

"I'm for that," agreed Fred, and soon the two men were consuming a man-sized breakfast. "Now," said Fred, "how can I help in the church? I want to get going in the Lord's work to make up for a lot of lost time." The pastor, still wary, parried the question by suggesting that they wait awhile to see what might develop. But Fred would brook no delay. "No, sir, I want to get at it. Let's turn the church and the town upside down for Jesus Christ."

"Well," said the pastor, bewildered by the vigorous new convert, "tell you what: I'll make you a member of the official board of the church. The board is meeting tonight. You be on hand and we will give you some kind of job in the church. What do you say to that?"

"O.K.," declared Fred, "that sounds pretty good. I'll be there tonight and let's get some action going." The exhausted pastor ushered his superenthusiastic nocturnal visitor out of the door and collapsed into a chair. "Brother," he asked himself, "what do I do with this guy now?"

That night at the board meeting Fred, not previously very interested in the church but now a board member, found his welcome a bit short of cordial. While the members were pleased to learn of his spiritual rebirth, they were still hesitant to accept him in church leadership. When the treasurer's report was given, it indicated an $11,000 deficit in the current expense budget of the church. Fred heard this news with disbelief and excited concern. "Why," he asked, "should the church of God operate at a deficit? It's incredible, disgusting. Something must be done about this at once. I will start by giving $1,000 to wipe out that deficit. Come on, now, you fellows, pony up like I'm doing." The response was negligible, the atmosphere cool.

But Fred was not daunted. "I'll raise that budget deficit in a few days," he said confidently, and proceeded to do just that by vigorous and positive calling throughout the community. Despite his perhaps overly enthusiastic and ill-advised aggressiveness, his sincerity and changed life became apparent and respected. He took hold of a sleepy and ineffective Sunday school class for teenagers. By his dynamic attitude, his zeal, and his with-it program dealing with matters of interest to young people, he soon built it into the largest and best-conducted class of its kind in the state.

Regularly he would bring his class down to New York to our Marble Collegiate Church to attend the service in a body. His manner of doing this was characteristic. He would get me on the telephone and announce, "Hey, Norman, I'm bringing a big gang of kids down Sunday night to hear you talk. So for heaven's sake have something on the ball, will you?" Thus prompted, I would indeed try to come up with something of a vital spiritual nature to match the powerful spiritual vitality of this tremendous person.

So the years passed and Fred creatively touched the lives of boys and girls in a manner quite unequaled. Once, on an airplane en route to Chicago, a young businessman sitting beside me apparently recognized me. "I owe everything that I am," he told me in a choked-up voice, "to dear old Fred R. What a guy! I love him, as do hundreds of other kids whom he saved. He certainly got me on the right track." Fred knew the joy and he had the power—the positive power of Jesus Christ. And others got it from him, and they got it good.

It all came about because someone cared enough to take him to a vital meeting and expose him to Christ. A preacher had a message that made sense, and he knew how to reach a mixed-up young man. And the man became a vigorous disciple, a memorable layman, a great teacher, a powerful motivator for Christ. He had the power and the joy.

HANG IN THERE

Some of the people I tell about in this book are living and some have gone on into the life beyond. I would like to come right out and use their names but have decided not to do so, for that could be an invasion of their privacy. Besides, a few readers might attempt to contact them, as has sometimes happened, and since this has in some cases proved embarrassing to quiet and reticent men and women, I have tried throughout the book, save in a very few instances, to avoid making identity clear. Every story in the book, however, is true in precise detail. Perhaps in recounting experiences of long ago, memory might not be altogether perfect, but in some cases I am able to draw upon records, and if not, the recall of the incident is possible in detail due to the powerful impression made upon me at the time.

One impression indelibly fixed in my mind is that strongly believing Christians are given power to hang in there when faced by harsh and formidable circumstances. I have long since decided that the fact that along with this indomitable power they also have joy indicates that the power and the joy are natural spiritual concomitants; they go together in a fundamental relationship. Christ makes good men and good women. He also makes strong men and strong women. Through faith they take on qualities of character that result in their becoming persons able to achieve victory in life, able to overcome, always to overcome. They become those glorious souls who at last are able to say: "I have fought a good fight, I have finished my course, I have kept the faith."[4]

On one occasion I had a visit with a former president of the United States, the late Herbert Hoover, for whom I personally had great admiration. His Christian faith and practice were profound. I asked him, "Mr. President, can you state in one sentence the secret of your success in life?" As quickly as the question was put, he answered, "With the help of God, I never gave up."

Captain Eddie Rickenbacker was one of the strongest human beings I ever knew. He was an authentic American hero. He was an indomitable personality; seemingly, nothing could ever defeat him. So I asked the

4. 2 Timothy 4:7

same question of him and he replied, "My mother, a very poor woman in Columbus, Ohio, taught her kids to pray, to read the Bible, to follow Jesus Christ and—never to give up."

Once Rickenbacker was in an airplane crash near Atlanta and was rushed to a hospital. It was thought he would die. He did, indeed, lie in and out of consciousness for a while. At that time one of the most famous radio commentators in the United States was the late Walter Winchell. In a broadcast he said, "Friends, pray for Eddie Rickenbacker. He is dying in an Atlanta hospital. He is not expected to live out the night." Rickenbacker was listening to the broadcast and when he heard this remark he grabbed a jug of water from his bedside and threw it at the radio, knocking it across the room, thus stopping the voice announcing that he was dying. He said, "I'm *not* going to die. I'm *not* going to give up."

This is the sort of no-defeat spirit that makes people great. Never give up! And when a person really achieves the never-give-up attitude, the power and the joy come through. "But," you say, "these are famous men; big shots, so to speak." But remember that a big shot is a little shot who keeps on shooting. The little shots who don't keep on shooting give up; hence they never become the big shots.

A nurse on the West Coast is a person of this type. She says in a letter:

> Many years ago I had an experience that I think was a miracle and you may publish it if you see fit. I am now an old lady, a retired nurse-anesthetist.
>
> I was practicing my profession in an industrial hospital owned by two doctors. Following two very hard falls, I developed a pain in my back and legs.

After months of agony I became paralyzed from my waist down. Organs were also affected. Several doctors were called in for consultation and a diagnosis of either cancer or lesion of the spine was made, which would mean I would never walk again.

I found out about the diagnosis and to me it was the end of everything. The outlook was so frightening I decided to end it all by committing suicide. To do this I figured out how to drag myself down to the surgery to my anesthetic gas machine, strap the mask on my face, and then turn on the nitrous oxide gas without any oxygen and it would be only a matter of a few seconds and it would be all over.

Well, the night I decided to do this I had to wait until the nurse made her rounds around 9 p.m. and while waiting for her I put on a small radio set that had been loaned to me. Now this is where I am sure a miracle happened.

The first and the only thing that came over the radio was a man's voice who said that at one time things were so tragic for him he decided to commit suicide. He tried seven different times. Each time something would happen to prevent him. The last and seventh time the thought came to him that if he couldn't stand this world, how did he know he could stand the other world. He concluded that the way to win in this or any world is simply never to give up.

I knew then that it was a direct message to me, so I decided to wait until after my operation, which was scheduled for the next day. The operation showed the cause of the paralysis was a blood tumor pressing against the spinal cord. The tumor was removed and after several months I took my first step. It took almost five years to be able to walk without a limp. I got a very good position and was helped in many ways and knew that the Lord had His hand in giving me courage and the "will" to carry on and never to give up. And a Scripture that helped me is Mark 9:23: " . . . If thou canst believe, all things are possible to him that believeth."

We have described the attitude of two famous men and a frail little old lady. But they all came out with the same result: no matter what happens to you, the important thing isn't what happens, but what you do about what happens to you. When discouraged or overwhelmed, if you have a sense of defeat, in the name of the Lord Jesus Christ who said that if you can only believe, nothing shall be impossible to you,[5] you need never give up. The power and the joy will be yours.

Just hang in there! Stick with it! Never give in to it! Stand up to your difficulties and face them head-on. When you do that you get victories, and when you begin to get victories your life will be tremendously enhanced. You will have a new sense of confidence, a new feeling of accomplishment, and boundless joy.

A minister friend of mine preached in churches in the Dakotas and in Montana, in what he called the great cattle country of the West. He told me that on one occasion he was attending an old cowboy, a tough, hard-bitten, weather-beaten old man off the plains. His skin was like leather and he had the bowlegs of a typical cowboy. He was a very good man, a righteous person, a dedicated member of a church, a humble servant of the Lord.

My friend sat with this cowboy on several occasions in his last illness, and one day he asked, "Jim, what did you learn in all your years on the plains herding cattle? Out there under the stars with the cattle, in the loneliness of the night, in the heat of summer and in the cold of winter, you must have learned something. What did you learn?"

The old cowboy considered for a moment, then said,

5. Matthew 17:20

"I learned to have great respect for the Hereford cattle. On the great plains there are violent snowstorms when the temperatures plunge below zero and the snow is driven by high winds. Most cattle would drift downwind and at a fence they would pile up and many would die. But it wasn't that way with the Hereford cattle. They wouldn't drift downwind. Instead, they forced themselves upwind and when they came to a fence or some kind of barrier they would huddle together, shoulder to shoulder; they would put their heads down and wait out the wind. And very few died from the elements.

"So," said the old cowboy, "I have learned that if you put your trust and faith in Almighty God, and walk every day with Jesus, and stand up to your difficulties when they come along, they will break on you and you will not break under them." If you can believe this—and it is logical and valid and the truth—if you can believe this, no matter what, nothing is going to be impossible unto you.

Of course trouble comes to everyone. Sometimes those who seem to laugh it off are those who have the worst troubles. Many people try to escape from their troubles in erroneous ways. Some attempt to drink themselves out of it. Others think they can run away from it. Some, futilely, just hope trouble will go away. But it is there and won't easily go away. What a real individual has to do is to just handle it by strong Christian belief.

COPYCAT

In making speeches and writing books, as I have been doing for a long time, one has some very interesting experiences with people. One time I was flying out to the West Coast. When we took off in New York I noticed that one man had several cocktails right away. The flight attendants are very careful about this kind of thing and usually they know how to control it, but this man was particularly difficult. He sat across the aisle from me and when he nodded to me, I nodded back to him; he did not know me, but he was in that state of being friendly with everyone by this time. I was correcting galley proofs of a book which I had just completed. Time was important because it was close to the publisher's deadline, and I had to go over the proofs word for word from beginning to end. In the five hours required to fly to the West Coast, I could just about do that.

So I was working at the task constantly. Finally the flight attendant said, "There is a seat up front alone. Would you like to sit there? No one will bother you, I'll see to that, and you can work undisturbed." I thanked her and went to the designated seat and was working diligently. But this man saw me and came up despite the efforts of the flight attendant. "Tell me," he said, "what in the world are you doing? The minute you boarded this airplane you started to work, and you've been working ever since. I never saw a man work so hard. What are you doing?"

"I'm correcting the galley pages of a new book."

"What is the name of the book?"

"It's called *The Positive Principle Today*."

"What is it about?" he persisted.

"It tells how positive thinking will work today just as it has always worked."

"Ah," he said, shaking a finger at me, "you are a

copycat. I know a guy back in New York who writes that kind of stuff and you're a copycat."

"What is the name of that man in New York?" I asked.

"His name is Norman Vincent Peale."

Then I attempted to tell him who I am, but he would not believe me. Actually, he made me show my driver's license to satisfy him as to my identity.

Then he changed to a serious mood. "Does this positive thinking really work?"

"It certainly does. I wouldn't be writing about it if it didn't."

"What is positive thinking?" he asked.

"It is faith in God, faith in Jesus Christ, faith in life, and faith in yourself."

"You know, you're talking to a tough guy. Right now I've got one of the roughest problems I ever had. I don't think I can get through it; I really don't think that I can. I believe it has me licked and I don't know what I'm going to do. I don't ordinarily drink this much," he declared. "The reason I've been drinking to this extent is that I want to forget my problems for a few hours, that's all. But I'm smart enough to know they will be waiting for me when I sober up. What ever am I going to do? I've got to admit that I am terribly afraid I don't have what it takes."

"Are you seriously asking for an answer," I asked, "or just talking?"

"Yes, I really am serious."

"O.K. Then I should like to ask if you believe in Jesus Christ."

"Oh, yes, certainly. I was brought up by Christian parents, good people."

"But have you ever committed your own life to Christ?" He asked me to explain just what that meant, and then said, "No, I never did that."

"I can tell you that if you will do that sincerely, you will no longer need any crutch. You will be given strength so that you will never think of giving up; you will be able to win out in whatever difficult circumstances you may face. Commit yourself totally to Christ; live His way, and you will have all the strength needed to stand up to your problems. I shall pray for you that you may come to know Christ personally, for that will make a great change in your life."

We parted in San Francisco Airport. I did not hear from this man, indeed did not see him again, until some months later he came up to me in a large crowd of people going into a convention meeting where I was scheduled to speak. He put his arm around my shoulder and said, "Do you remember the drunk on the airplane?"

"Which drunk?" I asked.

"Don't you remember the man who bothered you when you were working on that new book of yours, the guy who told you that you were a copycat?"

"Oh, it's you, is it? Glad to see you again."

"That witness about Christ you gave me, remember?"

"Yes, I remember."

"Well, it worked. I knew I was wrong. I knew you were right. Deep within me I had what it took to meet that situation and I knew I shouldn't be defeated or act weak, as I was doing. So I took your suggestion. I committed my life to Christ like you said. I asked Him to take over. As a result new insights came to me, new understanding. I felt strength, actually a feeling of power. I've never been so happy. Thanks a lot."

He had gotten the message and the spiritual experience was so clearly evident that I said to him, "Will you do me a favor in return for what you say I was able to do for you?"

"What's that?" he asked.

"I know that God will hear your prayers and I need a little help too, right now. How about you praying for me?"

"What do you know about that? You asking me to pray for you! Sure, I will. Thanks for asking me."

I felt the power and the joy in this airplane acquaintance and found myself reflecting on that great passage of Scripture, "If thou canst believe, all things are possible to him that believeth."[6]

So comes the power and with it the joy. And this creative experience, in whatever form, results from the positive power of Jesus Christ.

The joy of the redeemed life in Christ comes through in a letter from the Director of Public Affairs of the Police Department of one of America's largest cities, and with it I conclude this chapter, "The Joy and the Power."

> Dear Dr. Peale:
>
> I have been one of your followers for many years, have read (*and believed!*) all of your books. While I know that I am only one of many, many people whose lives your ministry has drastically changed, I still want to tell you how much I appreciate you, and thank you!
>
> A dear friend casually gave me *Positive Thinking* in the lobby area of a Lubbock, Texas, newspaper on a very cold, snowy day in 1958. Twenty years ago I read the book, and found it to be something I could accept and

6. Mark 9:23

act on. I have been acting on it ever since, and the principles have never failed me, although I have been through some dark days.

My life changed from a young man of nineteen who was habitually gloomy, depressed, and generally defeated into a life of hope, excitement, and expectation. I can honestly say that I have received all the things I really wanted from life, and it continues to be more fulfilling and exciting day by day.

Your messages helped me to find Jesus as a real person and Savior; because of your inspiration, I have found a full Christian life as a born-again believer. I give testimony to this fact every chance I get, and as you might suspect, I give you all the credit for leading me to a full and positive life and to my ultimate acceptance of Jesus as Lord and Master of my life.

I have been in police work for over ten years, and I thank God for the daily opportunities He gives me for witness and service. You would probably be surprised, I think, at the number of police officers who are finding a new way of life—a Jesus-filled life which creates in them a positive mental attitude and a rich existence.

Well, I have rambled much too much, and I could go on and on.

God bless you and keep you, Dr. Peale, and thank you again for what you are continuing to do for your fellowman.

Sincerely yours,
Tom H. Stevenson

9

Excitement and the Power

THE MORE COMPLETELY THE POWER TAKES HOLD of one, the more exciting life becomes. Indeed, it has been my observation that the power enhances the capacity to be excited. An in-depth spiritual experience inevitably brings an effervescent, though emotionally controlled, excitement. I have known dull and lethargic persons to come alive, astoundingly so, when they began living on a Christ-centered basis. People for whom life was only an uninspired routine of one thing after another suddenly became vital, even vibrant and excited about everything. They were actual demonstrations of the Scripture, "If any man be in Christ, he is a new creature."[1] Such persons began to "walk in newness of life,"[2] every day a new and thrillingly fresh experience. Everything for such persons became wonderfully different because they were themselves different when Christ took over within them. Even their awareness was sharpened to a keener sensitivity; excitedly they tell about ordinary light and color being enhanced, the songs of the birds sweeter, common things suddenly endowed with amazing beauty.

An example is the man who made an appointment with me to discuss his personal problems. He poured out a mass of negative and unhappy thoughts and fulminated bitterly on how "absolutely lousy everything and everybody is." He said he had made the appointment to get my advice, but instead of giving me a chance to do any advising he went into a tirade against the church and religion generally and preachers in particular. "How come you take the time to talk to me if you dislike preachers so much?" I asked.

"Oh, you are different," he replied. "You're not reli-

1. 2 Corinthians 5:17   2. Romans 6:4

gious; you're a positive thinker. And let me tell you, I'm not going to have anyone telling me that I need God. As a matter of fact, I hate God—if there is a God. So please tell me what I need to get some meaning out of this no-account life," he concluded dejectedly.

"God," I said.

"What's that you say?" he sputtered.

"God," I repeated. "You need God, for only He can straighten out the mess in your mind. Only God can give you healing and peace and joy, but He can do all that and more, that's for sure. You need God."

HE STOMPS OUT

The man glared at me and, jumping to his feet, shouted, "So, you are just like all the rest—just a God-talker! I thought you were a better educated, intelligent, and sophisticated man, same as I am."

"I guess you don't know what the word sophistication means," I interjected. "It means to know your way around in the world. Obviously you don't know your way around very well, for you are mixed up, hurt, and unhappy. So once again I say you need God."

My visitor apparently was angry with me, but perhaps even more so with himself. "God, God—always God," he muttered, and growling a short good-bye, he stomped out into the late afternoon winter darkness.

An hour later, just as I was about to leave my office in the church, my secretary called on the intercom. "That man is back, and he looks wild. Says he's just got to see you."

"All right, send him in." The man came rushing in and, indeed, he was rather wild-eyed and bewildered. "For God's sake," he exclaimed, "what has happened to me? Am I going nutty? Help me, Dr. Peale, please help me!" He told me a strange though not necessarily unique story. He said that when he stomped out of the church he turned to the right on 29th Street walking toward Broadway, muttering angrily, "God, God, that's all those fools know—God. God ——!" Then suddenly, to his astonishment, it seemed that everything was bathed in brilliant light; the drab streets became beautiful, as did the faces of people he passed. The sidewalks seemed to undulate and he felt that he was walking, or rather, floating upright above the sidewalks. He could not understand why passersby took no notice of him or the blinding light that enveloped him. He was uplifted, wondrously happy, and as light as air. But frightened also, and puzzled. Ah, he knew now. He had gone crazy.

He turned and rushed back to tell me about it and to implore help. "For God's sake, help me," he pleaded.

"You've said it," I replied. "It's for God's sake you have had this experience. God is calling you to Himself. He wants you to be His own. My friend, you have had a rare and marvelous experience of the mystical presence of God Himself such as is given to very few people. God must love you very much and believe in you to so reveal Himself."

He was stunned. I watched as he passed through kaleidoscopic emotions and a series of reactions. "It's unbelievable! Absolutely unbelievable! Even yet I feel. . ." he struggled for the word " . . . exalted, that's it—exalted! And clean—so clean. As though I had been washed. Fresh and clean. Everything is so very different. I never felt this way before."

"Some other people have," I told him. Then I took up a Bible and read to him about a similar experience that another and perhaps not too different type of man had once, a man named Saul of Tarsus, later called Paul, on the road to Damascus.

"But why me?" asked my visitor. "I'm not spiritual."

"The answer is that I don't know why," I replied. "But you can count on it that God has His reasons. As for not being spiritual, I can only say that you have just had an overwhelming spiritual experience. God will tell you what He wants of you if now, this very moment, you accept Jesus Christ as your Savior."

He nodded. "I do, indeed," and after a long silence he said, "I guess maybe that is what I've wanted for a long time and didn't realize it."

Again my visitor went out into the winter night, but this time as a very different person. He returned to Brooklyn and, as he later told me, spent a long time in prayer, during which guidance came that he was to dedicate his life to witnessing to the "intellectuals" with whom he associated. He himself was engaged in the international banking field and was a member, though not active, of Alcoholics Anonymous. He became outstandingly effective in bringing people to Christ who, because they had been so completely turned off, might never have known God had it not been for this remarkable man. His excitement for Christ was boundless, and he communicated an equally exciting new life to many others. The total occurrence was an impressive and unforgettable demonstration of the positive power of Jesus Christ.

As I have since considered this extraordinary story of life-changing, it was evident that at first this man was deeply hurting for lack of exuberance or zest in living. He was afflicted with a deadening case of ennui and even disgust with everything and everyone, including himself. Actually, he was starved for excitement. More and deeper life was his need. He was looking vaguely and inexpertly down the usual dead ends for that vibrant quality that makes life exciting. But when, through an astonishing circumstance, he encountered God and Jesus Christ, his life became filled with excitement, both within himself and outwardly toward life itself. He then proceeded to convey the inherent excitement of Christianity to all who had the good fortune to touch the activated personality of this reborn man.

NEED RETURN OF EXCITEMENT

It could very well be that a weakness in contemporary Christianity is a lack of excitement. In too many instances it does nothing to thrill, to challenge; too often it has settled down into dull desultoriness, as though old and tired. A powerful infusion of new and vibrant enthusiasm for Christ, for the church, for the Kingdom of God, and for individuals, with all the excitement of a tremendous crusade, would, I am sure, draw thousands to Christianity's banners. As it is, the quiet, overly traditional, deadly dull spirit, or lack of spirit, in most churches impresses modern people, if they think of it at all, as marking a once-great institution that has had its day. The great, thunderous epochs in Christian history are but as the old, faint, far-off bugle calls of heroic events faded into the past. It is sadly reminiscent of the story told by the famous writer James M. Barrie of a would-be author who asked him to suggest a title for a book he had written. "Any drums in it?" Barrie asked.

"No drums," replied the man, surprised.

"Any trumpets in it?"

"No, sir, no trumpets."

"Then," said Sir James matter-of-factly, "call it 'No Drums, No Trumpets.'"

There were times in the past when Christianity had plenty of drums and trumpets, and its glorious, ringing challenges drew youth by the hundreds of thousands. I recall great leaders like John R. Mott, Sherwood Eddy, and others who went everywhere talking to young people in a nationwide organization called Student Volunteers. Youth was being summoned to what virtually amounted to a worldwide crusade for Christ. This was at a time when I was in the throes of planning my own future and was rejecting the ministry for the newspaper business. At this juncture I went to a Student Volunteer convention in the old Memorial Hall in Columbus, Ohio.

Entering the building into which huge throngs of college students were pouring, I stopped short; stretching across the platform was a big banner with letters two feet high which read, "Let's Win the World for Christ in This Generation." That slogan struck me a powerful blow in the mind, or as they say now, "blew my mind." What wonderful audacity! What a magnificent and thrilling concept! I went for it with all I had of devotion, as did hundreds of thousands. I can remember yet that vast audience of students thunderously singing "Onward, Christian soldiers! . . . Like a mighty army moves the Church of God." But, alas, that day has receded into the past. Now, happily, there is an exciting new resurgence of youth movements for Christ. Youth still wants something of the same "Come on, let's get out there and change the world" spirit.

An exciting, completely Christ-centered Christianity possesses an enormous in-depth appeal. In this era of increased psychological knowledge of the responses of human beings, it is astonishing that the church has not made more appropriate uses of the quality of excitement. To do so would not need to do violence to reason and education. I recall sitting at a dinner one time with Dr. Roy Moore, an outstanding physician and surgeon, whom I had always thought of as rather aloof and unemotional. We were listening to Dr. John R. Mott, mentioned earlier, who now was an old man but still vigorous and enthusiastic.

Suddenly, to my surprise, I noticed that Dr. Moore was listening enthralled to the great old missionary leader and that tears were running down his face. When the speaker had finished Roy said, "He got to me when I was a student at Yale with his mentally sound, heart-moving call to follow Christ. After all these years he still reaches me with his reasoned presentation and enthusiasm. He made discipleship then so exciting, just as he does now. I was eager to follow Jesus anywhere." He turned to me. "Norman," he said, "you do the same to me. You move me. Because you are excited, I stay excited." I remember his statement with gratitude, for personally I have always been tremendously excited about Jesus. Indeed, my whole positive approach is based on a strong faith in Jesus Christ and an intense desire to persuade everyone whom I can possibly influence to likewise become excited about Him.

HE BECAME AN EXCITED CHRISTIAN

Persuading men and women that the Christlike life is the exciting life is evidenced by a letter, out of many thousands of similar type, from Don Sutaria, a deeply

Christ-committed member of my church. Don writes as
follows:

My dear Dr. Peale:

You were God's instrument in leading me to Christ.
My chronological age is 38, but as a "born again"
Christian, I am only one year old today—kicking, and
growing, and having fun in this beautiful world. I accepted Christ as my personal Lord and Savior during
your Easter Sunday message of "forgiveness and love"
last year. And it was one of the happiest days of my life.
There is no turning back now.

Dr. Peale, may God bless you and Mrs. Peale for
what you have done in my life and my wife's life spiritually. We pray for both of you often.

My wife accepted Christ during Lent four years ago.
I was slow in accepting Christ. I read all your books and
listened regularly to your sermons at Marble Collegiate
Church for twelve years (that's a pretty long time . . .
eh!). My hangups were primarily intellectual and cul-
tural. This was partially because I was raised as a Parsee
Zoroastrian in Bombay, India, until I was twenty-three.
But the good Lord's timing is perfect! And here I am
now, a growing Christian. My conversion was not easy.
I am working on my newfound Christian way of life,
every day.

One of your sermons really inspired me—I have
made it my personal philosophy of life. I had pasted
these words on my bedside bureau, next to the alarm
clock, so that I saw them every day when I opened my
eyes, first thing in the morning. These words are:

"THINK POSITIVE"
"DO THE VERY BEST YOU CAN"
"PUT YOUR FAITH IN GOD (CHRIST)"
"PRAY"
"LET GO (RELAX)"

How about the "Morning Treatment". . .

I still use it:

"In The Beginning God"
"Walk in Newness of Life"
"This is the Day that the Lord Hath Made, Let Us
    Rejoice and Be Glad in It"
"I Believe, I Believe, I Believe"
"I Feel Healthy, I Feel Happy, and I Feel Terrific"

In addition to that, we have family devotionals every morning from "Daily Guideposts," and grace at family mealtimes. In addition, "Flash Prayers" throughout the day also help. I tell you, Dr. Peale, we rarely have very tough days, maybe two or three a year.

My "Midday Treatment" consists of reading "Thought Conditioners," or parts of *The Living Bible*, or a chapter or two from *The Power of Positive Thinking*, or the FCL booklet, *What the Bible Tells the Businessman*, or "Pocket Cards." I have enjoyed giving away copies of these books and booklets as gifts to various friends and acquaintances, and witnessing the gospel to them.

I came to these marvelous United States of America as a graduate student. I did not know a soul and I did not have a dime—just borrowed money ($6,000) for education. But now with God's help and through the power of Christ, I am an American citizen, married to a happy, beautiful, loving and smart wife, Betty, and have a three and a half year old chirpy son. Guess what we named our son . . . he is named Norman as a measure of our love and honor for you.

You know, on my desk at work, I have the Bible and *The Power of Positive Thinking* (with all Bible passages and other relevant material underlined . . . and I refer to it at least once every day). I also have a copy of *The Power of Positive Thinking* next to my bed at home; it was autographed by you when you came one Sunday evening to talk with the Marble Young Adults where I was a member. You gave some "helpful hints" to young singles at that talk in terms of priorities in life and marriage. Brother, did it affect me. . . . I met my wife at a church nearly ten years ago and we were married a year and a half later. We even came to the Sunday evening get-together of the Marble Young Adults—the first day we met. Isn't that terrific!!!

My thinking and acting has really changed from mildly negative to strongly positive, and I give your book, *The Power of Positive Thinking*, all the credit. I picked it up one night thirteen years ago at Walgreen's Drug Store in the Port Authority building. I was feeling depressed over a broken love affair. That weekend I read the book several times, and on Monday morning I felt like a new and different person. During these thirteen years, I have given away to friends at least twice as many copies of this book.

I am bursting at the seams with happiness. It is hard to compress thirteen years of appreciation and affection for you in one letter. But you have given me a deep religious faith in Christ, something which no one can take away. So thanks again.

God has such a fantastic plan for our life, if we only trust Him! I now work for a superb company, I have a good boss, and we even have a Bible study once a week during lunch break. Isn't that wonderful!

May God bless you and Mrs. Peale richly, and keep you in your inspirational pulpit for many years to come . . . this is our humble and heartfelt prayer.

> Your spiritual friend and brother-in-Christ,
> Don

That letter from Don Sutaria is filled with genuine enthusiasm for the Lord and His work, and it coincides with my own enthusiastic attitudes, both when I was young and concurrently now. When Jesus Christ came into my life everything was wondrously new and fresh. There was a lift to my whole nature and a lilt in all my emotional reactions. I became excited, terrifically excited, by the basic fact of being alive and in this wonderful world, eager to do all possible to help people find the same great thing that had come into my life—the positive power of Jesus Christ.

DOWN MEMORY LANE

My wife and I were in Boston for a couple of TV programs to talk about a new book which I had just published. We were staying in a hotel opposite Boston Common and overlooking the public gardens. Have you ever taken a trip backward into the past? Well, I did just that, standing in our room on the fourteenth floor of the hotel, looking out the window. The view was over the Common toward Beacon Street and Beacon Hill and the State House. It was on Beacon Hill where I studied for three years at the School of Theology. I worked my way through, in part, by working in a restaurant on Beacon Street. The brownstone buildings up and down that street still looked the same after all those years. One of them was the YWCA, and it was here that I worked. The restaurant was on the third floor and the kitchen in the basement. A fellow-student and I earned our meals and a couple of dollars a week each for operating the dumbwaiter, he at the top and I at the bottom of the shaft. He would yell down, "Send up . . . " whatever the order was, and I would comply. Then he would send the used dishes down to me. As operators of the dumbwaiter, it was said all around that we were two of the dumbest waiters they ever had in that restaurant!

From the hotel room I could also see the very walks we used to cross Boston Common, talking about what? The glorious future we were going to have preaching the gospel of the Lord Jesus Christ! We were studying on Beacon Hill because we had been fired with the conviction that God had called us to go out and help people in Christ's name, to lift them up out of themselves, to get them to stop doing bad and start doing good, to change their attitude from negative to positive, to lead them to be committed followers of Christ. And we were enthused about the ministry.

I can remember yet how excited we were in those days on Beacon Hill and on Beacon Street and on Boylston Street and in the public gardens and Boston Common. Looking out the window that day after all those years, I could almost see a young man twenty years old striding across that Common. He was an excited fellow in those days. Why was he excited? Because he had known a personal, transforming, saving experience of God in his life, and he had given himself to the Lord. Then God called him to go out into the world and use his meager talents to try to help people in the name of Christ.

So here he was, many years after he ran that dumbwaiter, looking out of a hotel window into the past, and he asked himself if he still had the same enthusiasm. "Have you still got this positive attitude? Do you still possess this excitement? Are you still dedicated to the faith?" Praise the Lord, I could say, "Yes!"

Why was it possible to say yes? Because in my own way I try to do my simple, dead-level best to live with Him and to be what He wants me to be. When you do that honestly and sincerely, then the power comes— and it never leaves if you do not leave the Master. I haven't done anything great, but I have tried to serve Christ. I can state with certainty that you can keep the excitement going all your life if you keep the positive power going always.

A good example is the handyman who works in our

apartment house in New York. When he comes up to fix something for me, we often have a bit of a talk. He had been trying to find the Lord. One day he said, "What do you know! I was walking on Madison Avenue at 84th Street when all of a sudden there was a tremendous feeling of joy in my heart like nothing I had ever known before. What do you suppose happened to me?"

"I can tell you what happened to you," I replied. "You found Him and He found you."

"I am happier than I've ever been in my life! I'm really excited."

"Thank God," I said. "Keep it going. Always keep it going. Never lose that excitement." In whatever way you find the presence of God in your own life, by whatever method, by whatever form or symbol, hold on to it. Stay with it. Keep always spiritually alive and excited.

It is possible to stay perpetually alive, constantly enthusiastic, always excited. The method for doing so is to live all day every day in the company of Christ. As you walk with Him your thoughts are clean and good and loving, your attitudes unselfish and outgoing. You have the feeling of being right with God, with other people, and right with yourself. Your life takes on glorious meaning that is not obscure or fuzzy but clear and definite. Day follows day with anticipation and hope and faith.

Years pass with all their many problems, but the spirit is never dulled. You never become disillusioned or apathetic or blasé or tired, for you are constantly being renewed in the spirit by drinking the bubbling, effervescing fountains of the water of life. You catch yourself saying those glorious lines from Tennyson: "O, I see the crescent promise of my spirit hath not set/Ancient founts of inspiration well thro' all my fancy yet."[3] It is a fact, a great, big, marvelous fact, that "In him was life; and the life was the light of men."[4] This does not mean, of course, that you will experience no trouble, no pain or suffering; for you will. Even so, you have the built-in upthrust that lifts you above all of it forever. Always you have the positive power of Jesus Christ going for you to insure victory and then again victory. Hence the perpetuity of the excitement factor in the life of the committed Christian.

PRACTICE BEING EXCITED TO BE EXCITED

I have been most fortunate in life to have had as friends some very exciting people. One of them whose memory I revere was Grove Patterson, one-time editor of the *Toledo Blade*, a famous newspaper executive, great writer, and dynamic Christian. I worked for him as a reporter on the old *Detroit Journal* and he became a lifelong friend from whom I learned much.

When fresh out of college I went to work for him. "Have you had any experience in journalism?" he asked.

"Oh, yes," I replied. "I was associate editor of my college paper." Whereupon he told me to repeat after him the statement, "I know nothing at all about journalism," which I proceeded meekly to do. He then said he was going to give me a lesson in writing. With his pencil he put a dot on a sheet of white paper. "Know what that is?" he asked.

"It's a dot," I said.

"No, it is a period, the greatest literary device known

3. from poem, "Locksley Hall."   4. John 1:4

222

to man. When you have finished a sentence—and always make it a short sentence—put down a period. Never run on and on. Always make your story interesting, factual, and honest. Tell only the truth. Be a reliable reporter and writer. Use short words, a simple yet graphic style, and be succinct. Let us say that you have two readers—one a digger of ditches and the other a university professor. To which will you write? To the less educated, of course; the better educated will understand.

"Now, son," he said one day, "I detect some self-doubt in you." Apparently my old inferiority complex was showing through. "You seem to come to this office rather dispirited from time to time, as though you were discouraged or even unhappy. For what it may mean to you, I have never had a low moment since one night years ago."

"What happened then?" I asked curiously, for I respected this man highly and grew to love him devotedly. His answer was simple and straightforward, as were all his comments. "I met Jesus Christ that night, and I've been happy and excited ever since. I have had plenty of ups and downs, but He lifted me up from the downs. He is a great Companion. You will never really be dispirited if you stick with Him." So saying, he got up out of his chair, came around the desk, and hit me a kindly whack on the back. "Get out there and enjoy being a reporter," he said, "and remember this: if you practice being excited you will be excited. Make it a habit. People will like you for it, and you will become a great newspaperman."

I explained that I, too, had experienced conversion and was a committed Christian. "It's a matter of depth," he declared. "Surrender to Christ and acceptance of

Him as Lord and Savior can give you release from sin and weakness, but to get full joy and the excitement you must let Christ take over in every aspect of your life until no area is left unclaimed by Him, and then the deeper power will come. You apparently still have some fears and some inadequacy feelings. Let them all go by, putting yourself totally into the Lord's hands."

FROM REPORTER TO MINISTER

Throughout this period I was struggling within myself because I felt that God was calling me to the ministry. But I was resisting it. Under Mr. Patterson's guidance newspaper work was becoming a thrilling occupation. As a minister's son, my memories of some of the unpleasant things about the ministry—ecclesiastical maneuvering, dictatorial laymen, the tendency of some ministers to compel you to think as they did—had turned me off, at least partially. However, having committed myself always to obey God's will and loving Jesus Christ deeply, I felt that, for whatever strange reason I was being called, it was my duty as a Christian to follow the leading of the Holy Spirit.

Accordingly, I went in to tell Mr. Patterson that I had decided, after much agonizing prayer, that God wanted me to preach the gospel and that henceforth his paper would have to struggle along as best it could without my valued service! I thought he bore up right well, but the fact remains that I had not been gone from the *Detroit Journal* but a year or so before it merged with another paper. Mr. Patterson always contended that the departure to the ministry of his young reporter had no connection with the paper's demise.

Mr. Patterson congratulated me upon what he seriously took to be a valid call from God, although he was kind enough to express regret that I was giving up newspaper work. "There will always be printer's ink on your fingers," he warned. Apparently he was right, for I have written twenty-four books, had a national magazine column, write two newspaper columns currently, as well as publish *Guideposts* magazine, now the fourteenth largest publication in the United States with eleven million readers monthly.

"Remember those principles I gave you for writing a newspaper story," Mr. Patterson advised. "Keep your sermon interesting, use words everyone can understand, be succinct, be factual and honest, and put down a period when finished. Those rules apply to sermons as well as to newspaper writing. There is one additional principle that is vital; always be excited—and why not, for you will be talking about the greatest truth in the world; you will be telling people that God loves them and Jesus saves them." In concluding he gave me this comfort: "If you don't like the ministry or don't do very well at it, come on back to the paper. Your old job will always be waiting for you."

One Sunday early in my long service at Marble Collegiate Church in New York City I looked down from the pulpit and noticed Grove Patterson in the congregation. With my usual strong desire to persuade people about the things of God, I was excitedly talking about the greatness of Jesus and what He can do for anyone. Afterward, as I greeted people in front of the pulpit, along came my old editor. I felt that even if he had to stretch the point a bit he might say something nice about his erstwhile reporter's sermon. Instead, with a dour look he said, "Well, Norman, your old job is still waiting for you!"

Afterward in my study he sat back in an easy chair. "Norman," he said, "you moved me in that sermon by talking straight and simply about God and loving people and about how Jesus can take a surrendered life and make it wonderful. And you were sincere and honest. What you said is so practical, sensible, and down to where people live. You meant every word you said. You were excited and enthusiastic and as a result the power came through. I felt it deeply. Never lose that excitement."

The last time I ever saw this great human being was when we sat together one night on a platform which had been erected in the middle of the Cotton Bowl at Dallas, Texas. He presented me to the crowd of 75,000 persons. As he turned from the podium and I stepped forward to speak, he said, "Make the good old gospel exciting and the power will come down in this huge crowd." I learned much about the positive power of Jesus Christ from Grove Patterson, top newspaper editor, public speaker extraordinary, magnificent Christian, and beloved friend.

Perhaps Grove, looking down from above, may have been with me in spirit one night not long ago when the president of Sales and Marketing Executives International surprisingly presented me with that organization's Salesman of the Year Award. He explained why this highly regarded award was given to a preacher. A salesman persuades, and in the end he sells because of what he is. A true salesman is sincere, honest, factual, and always enthusiastic. He truly wants to help his customer. All these are the same principles Grove taught.

My response to the first presentation of this award to a preacher dwelt on the honor I felt in being given this recognition, especially since I am not thought of as a salesman. Then the definition of selling given by an old friend of mine, Millard Bennett, came to mind. He was a very successful salesman, and defined salesmanship as "the use of sincere and enthusiastic persuasion by which another person is induced to walk a road of agreement with you." What better description could apply to those of us who spend our lives sincerely and enthusiastically persuading men and women to walk a road of agreement that Jesus Christ is the way, the truth, and the life?[5]

ARE PEOPLE STILL BEING CONVERTED?

There was a time when I was under rather considerable attack, primarily by some ministers, strangely enough, simultaneously from the left of middle and the right of middle point of view. They roundly condemned me for my book, *The Power of Positive Thinking*, for a variety of reasons: it was not written in accepted religious language, it was a "how to get rich" success book, it had ideas different from those currently in vogue among the church hierarchy, and the book was having an extraordinarily large sale. This attack was often on something called "Pealeism," which I presume was a composite of the above.

One man, a church official (not a pastor of a church but a minister), was particularly bitter toward me. While I had never met him, he had rather unkind things of a personal nature to say about me. About this time he, too, had written a book and I was asked by the editor of a periodical to review it. It was an excellent book, well written, and while it presented a point of view with

5. John 14:6

which I had some disagreement, I felt it basically was worth a favorable review, which I proceeded to produce. It so happened that this man found it necessary to see me about a certain matter, and I felt he was under some strain of embarrassment as he sat in my office. "Thank you," he said, "for your favorable review of my book. I was surprised that you spoke so well of it, considering all the things you must know I have said about you."

"The matter under consideration was your book," I said, "and not your attitude toward me. I thought highly of your book."

He shook his head. "Still, it was pretty decent of you not to take it into account."

"I've always tried to be objective," I said, "though I'm certainly anything but a saint."

Then followed one of the strangest interviews of my ministry, which has known many surprising encounters. We discussed the matter that had brought us together; then the man began to talk about our Institutes of Religion and Health in which a team of pastors, psychologists, and psychiatrists pool their expertise in dealing with human problems. Sort of laughingly he said he guessed he ought to become a patient, for he was completely exhausted, irritable, and all the zest and excitement he had possessed at one time had now "gone down the drain." He paused, then asked, "You're an expert in this field. Why does a man run out of enthusiasm and go around with a fed-up feeling and everything leaving a bad taste in his mouth?"

"Oh, I'm no expert," I replied, "though we do have experts on our staff. We use psychiatrists to help us understand what happens to people mentally and emotionally, and some have been healed by the therapy of psychological medicine. But I am one of those who prefer to bring new life to people by the powerful therapy of the gospel."

"You mean you still believe that people, like me, for example, can be healed by the gospel, and does anyone actually get converted anymore?" I was surprised but deeply moved that he seemed to say this rather wistfully. "Oh, yes, indeed, they certainly do, and through conversion they find a wonderful and exciting new life," I replied.

My visitor sat as if in deep thought. "Look," he said, "I know you don't like me and I haven't liked you, but I'm going to humble myself and ask you to help me because, in spite of everything I have said, I think you are a sincere man of God."

I thanked him and stated that he was wrong about one thing; I did not dislike him. "I try to be like Will Rogers, who said, 'I never met a man I didn't like,'" I told him, and expressed my desire to help him if I could. "How do you go about being converted and finding that peace and joy you refer to?" he asked. I said that the requirements were the confession of sin, an expression of belief in the power of Christ to heal the lesions of the mind and soul, acceptance of Christ as Lord and Savior, a humble request for forgiveness, and the willingness to turn oneself completely over to God.

I could hardly believe my ears when he asked if I would hear his confession. Managing to conceal my astonishment in a professional manner, I said, "It will be an honor to do so, especially since I see you as a strong, honest man sincerely wanting your life to be changed. Let's go into the church," I suggested. In the half-darkened and quiet sanctuary this intelligent and brilliant man emptied his mind and bared his soul to God. We prayed on the basis of the two: "If two of you shall agree on earth as touching any thing that they shall ask, it shall be done for them of my Father which is in heaven."[6]

I said, "My friend, as a, shall we say, doctor of the soul, I have called in at your request the Great Physician of soul, mind, and body. You have humbly confessed your sins to Him. He has forgiven them. They are now blotted out, separated from you as far as the east is from the west.[7] 'Though your sins be as scarlet, they shall be as white as snow,'"[8] I reminded him. "Now forgive yourself and enter into the fullness of life in Christ."

With a new look on his face—I thought of it at the time as an astonished look—he said, "What has happened to me is simply the great old faith. It still has the power. What a relief! I feel like a new man."

Indeed he was a new man. He found the peace of mind that he had lost; the old enthusiasm returned. He told me later that he even attained a quality of physical health and well-being that he had not enjoyed for months. He continued a happy man until his death some years later. He found the power, and with it an excitement in his life and work that he never lost again. He still continued to take issue with me now and then, which, he averred, was "good for my soul." But his treatment of me was loving in a gruff sort of way.

REMADE BY THE POWER
It has been my privilege and opportunity to speak regularly on radio for over forty years, both nationally and on two New York stations. The sermon exactly as

6. Matthew 18:19   7. Psalm 103:12   8. Isaiah 1:18

preached in the church on Sunday morning is aired the same evening from 6:45 to 7:15 o'clock. It is a favorable time since thousands of people are driving on the highways of the New York metropolitan area at that hour and the number of listeners in automobiles is very great. It is aired at other times on other stations across the nation. Many persons have told me that my type of preaching has made Christ a reality to them, and I have even considered a book dealing with life-changing stories that have resulted solely from radio talks. These stories are many, and very moving indeed. But let me tell you just one of them.

Jack was a salesman and had plenty of ability, but he wasn't doing too well, due to his gambling and drinking habits. Long nights out on the town left him less than fit for competitive selling, and the gambling, which seldom turned in his favor, had adversely affected his economic situation. In a word, and more simply expressed, he was close to being broke. Accordingly, his personal situation was, as he later described it, "in pretty much of a mess."

Naturally his spirit took a beating, and from a normally positive and enthusiastic person he became increasingly discouraged, despondent, and morose. He fully realized that he was on a downhill skid both professionally and personally, but did not seem to have the inner force to put a stop to the ruinous course he was on. So he drifted in a continuing downward spiral until early one Sunday morning the positive power of Jesus Christ reached him.

After an all-night gambling session, he was returning to his home in Greensboro, North Carolina, when he turned on the car radio. A man was talking and the first words Jack heard were these: "No matter how bad your situation or how you have messed up your life, you can move up to better things beginning, not tomorrow or next week or next year, but now, this very day. All you need do is to want to change yourself enough to take one step, and that one step will lead to a vast improvement in your situation."

This sort of talk made sense to Jack. It clearly stated a fact. He was in trouble; and it promised the possibility of a way out, which sounded like another fact. When the speaker suggested that the one step was to repeat a statement and believe that it could work this miracle, Jack was half-convinced. But then doubt began to creep into his mind. "This guy talks straight, but he will probably turn out to be a preacher, even though he doesn't sound preachy," he thought to himself. He had tuned into the program late and had not heard the speaker's name.

Apparently the speaker must have been aware of the possibility of a doubting reaction, for he said, "Now, some of you may be saying, 'This man sounds like a preacher,' and you are fixing to turn me off. Don't do that, because if you are in real trouble there is a way out and up for you if you are smart enough to go for it. The statement that can work a miracle in your life is this, and I will give it to you slowly. Suppose you repeat it along with me." Despite himself, Jack found he was going along with the speaker as he stated the words, "I can do all things through Christ."[9]

Jack pulled to the side of the road. He knew that what he had just heard was the truth about the condition he was in and also about the way out of that unhappy condition. Sitting by the roadside he prayed to Jesus for

9. Philippians 4:13

help, and his prayer brought him a strange and exciting sense of peace. When he started his car and turned back onto the highway he was on God's highway, and it took him to a better life than he had ever dreamed possible.

Some weeks later I was in Greensboro on a speaking engagement, and our southern *Guideposts* representative, Charles Kennard, asked if he could bring a man to see me who had experienced a spiritual rebirth as a result of one of my radio talks. It was Jack, and he told me the preceding story. His sincerity and enthusiasm came through, and we prayed that God would guide him across all the future years. It seemed to me that God had most certainly saved Jack for something big.

Eighteen years passed. Only a few months ago, as I sat in a dressing room backstage at the Kansas City Convention Center, a rap came at the door and a fine-looking man entered, accompanied by his wife. I was one of five speakers scheduled to speak at a meeting billed as a "Positive Thinking Rally," and a capacity audience of some 15,000 persons was expected. My visitor told me he was minister of a large church and he was to open the meeting that day with prayer.

"But I would not be here today, nor would I be a minister," he said, "had it not been for you. Once, years ago, I told you how you helped me."

"Please tell me again, as I cannot recall our meeting," I said. He started to tell the story, then I stopped him. "You are Jack, and I met you in a motel in Greensboro, North Carolina, a long time ago." Then ensued fifteen minutes of fellowship and spiritual praise.

Later this erstwhile gambler delivered a prayer that deeply moved that great audience. It was not a perfunctory type of invocation so often delivered at such gatherings. Instead it was a happy, humble, but enthusiastic affirmation of how great life can be when you are on the highway to the future with Christ leading every day all the way. In the Kansas City auditorium that spring day I saw demonstrated once again the excitement and romance of the positive power of Jesus Christ.

10

Strength
and the Power

STRENGTH! IT IS SORELY NEEDED BY YOU AND BY me, indeed by every mortal on earth. Soon or late, and often when least expected, the critical need is for strength. And strength is supplied by the power, the positive power of Jesus Christ.

I know these statements to be true because of their application to a profound family crisis that developed one Sunday evening for Ruth and me. Since a mother can perhaps talk about such things in a deeper way, I am asking her to tell you about a time we needed strength that only the power could supply and which it did in full measure:[1]

> It was a Sunday that had been a happy day from morning until night, and then—! After church we went to lunch with some friends and had a relaxed and enjoyable visit. The day was, you might say, one grand, sweet song. In the afternoon we did some other interesting things and finally got home about seven P.M. to find a message to call a surgeon at the North Carolina University Hospital in Chapel Hill.
>
> Our son, John, was completing his studies for a doctorate of philosophy degree at the university. We made the call. The surgeon said, "Your son came into this hospital today in an emergency, suffering great agony. We've tested him throughout the afternoon and we've arrived at a diagnosis of inflamed gallbladder with probably pancreatic complications." He continued, "We're medicating him, trying to delay operating, because he has a hot gallbladder [that's what he called it]. It's dangerous to operate with the gallbladder in this condition. We hope to reduce the infection and bring down his temperature first and operate on him later."
>
> "Well, doctor," I said, "he is in your hands and he is in God's hands. You do what you think is best." We immediately went into prayer, praying for the doctor,

1. From *The Adventure of Being a Wife,* by Ruth Stafford Peale

praying for our only son. At 11:15 that night the doctor called back and said, "John hasn't responded to medication. The situation is becoming very serious. I do not like to operate under these conditions—it's dangerous to operate; but it's more dangerous not to. So I must operate."

Again I said, "Doctor, he is in your hands and in God's hands. Dr. Peale and I will be with you in prayer. Bring him through for us."

"I'll try mighty hard," he said.

So then we faced each other. This is our only son. We knew he was in great danger. But all our lives we have practiced to the best of our ability the idea of letting go and letting God. It is very hard to let go of your own son when everything within you draws him to yourself, but I believe we achieved it.

The doctor had said he would call us back in about two to three hours, that being the time he thought the operation would require.

But he didn't call us back. Four hours passed; then five hours. Six hours went by. We literally prayed all night long. Even though no word had come from the surgeon, at about 3:30 in the morning I had a strong conviction that it was going to be all right with John and that I could leave him in the hands of God. I told this to Norman. He said, "I had the same feeling a few moments ago."

At six o'clock in the morning the doctor called. He said, "I'm glad to report that John came through the operation successfully. He's a very sick boy, but he is also a good healthy boy. He has lived a clean life, and that counts when the chips are down. I feel that he will be all right."

Not in years have I had so great a sense of the greatness and the goodness and the love of God as I did that night.

Later I learned that at about three A.M. the situation became so serious that they brought the hospital's chief surgeon in to take part in the operation. I also told the doctor I had been praying for my son all night. He said, "I always try to work in partnership with God."

In this deeply human crisis, which occurs in every family in one form or another, we learned once again that you can trust this thing called guidance. Through the positive power of Jesus Christ, strength came in crisis.

STRENGTH TO KEEP GOING

Simply to keep going can sometimes become a problem. This is true not only when the going gets hard, but when it is necessary to sustain the continuous demands of responsibility. A mother who has very little money and is forced to work and mend and cook and clean day in and day out surely needs resources of strength upon which to draw. This is true at all levels of activity. With business people, the combined responsibility of executive leadership and the hard fact of decision-making, which can have far-reaching effects upon the jobs of hundreds of people, bring many stresses. Such authority often causes people in business to crack up and suffer nervous breakdown. Such was the case of a man who sent his business card into my office after a church service one Sunday.

The name was that of a prominent business leader whom I had never met personally. We had a little talk at that time, and arranged to meet within a few days.

He explained in the interview that he was the president and chief executive officer of a large corporation; indeed, I knew it to be one of the largest in the country. He had arrived at this position because he had decision-making ability, and by far the greater number of his decisions had been wise ones. But now he had made several moves one after another that were unfortunate and two or three of them had been quite disastrous. He had

become sleepless worrying over decisions and conse-
quently was tired and lacking in energy. "I have completely run out of strength," he declared, "and in fact at
times have to push myself forcibly even to keep going."

This man told me that for some time he had been
regularly attending services at our church and that he
believed in what he termed "the practical and positive
gospel." He had been faithfully practicing the principles
and techniques of faith taught in our church and not
without results. But now he felt, as he put it, that he
"needed some special personal treatment," and though
he was "reluctant to bother so busy a man," wondered
if he could get a "personal prescription especially designed" for him. He explained this seemingly unusual
request by reminding me that when he was ill physically he would go to a doctor and get a prescription
marked personally for him, Walter T., and was told
how and when to take it. He pointed out that I, too,
was a doctor, and would I give him a personal prescription for his spiritual and emotional condition. This effi-
cient approach taught me something about the qualities
by which a man rises to top leadership. "Give me something I can take and do to keep me going, to help me
think and decide right," he demanded. "Give me some
spiritual medicine that will restore my strength."

This prominent industrialist had given me a pretty
tough order, but as he sat before me I realized that he
was a humble and believing man who was in trouble. I
further realized that he looked upon me, a pastor, with
the same confidence and respect that he would a doctor
of medicine. He was simply a patient who wanted the
medicine that would heal and he fully believed that I
knew what it was and how to administer it to him.

I assured him that we would do as he asked and would guarantee the results if he promised to believe implicitly and take the medicine precisely as directed. This, of course, was going out on a limb, but because of my own faith I was prepared to do just that. In this case I was aware of the mental caliber of the man with whom I was dealing. He was not fooling, nor was he vague. He wanted help and meant to get it. I knew he was very open to the work of the Holy Spirit, and I wasn't about to impede the Holy Spirit by putting qualifications and doubts in the way.

"Before I write the prescription for you," I said, "please answer these questions: Do you believe in God the Father?"

"Yes, I do," came the reply.

"Do you accept Jesus Christ as your Lord and Savior?"

"With all my heart," he answered fervently.

"And do you accept the Bible as the Word of God?"

"I do most certainly."

"And when I give you what we are calling a 'spiritual prescription' or guidance, will you prayerfully carry it out?"

"You give it to me, Dr. Peale, and I will give it all I have, sincerely and earnestly."

"O.K.," I said, and taking paper I wrote at the top, "Spiritual prescription for Walter T. to be taken as directed," and signed it "Norman Vincent Peale, Doctor of Divinity." That latter designation, which I never use, was to make it appear more official. He carried this prescription in his wallet for many years, and once when he showed me that "Norman Vincent Peale, Doctor of Divinity," I was a bit embarrassed. "Don't be," he said.

"It was the most scientific and effective prescription I ever received. You're a doctor, all right. And I should know, for you made me well."

"Oh, no, Walter, not I, but the Great Physician, Jesus."

"Yes, of course," he agreed. "You and I both know the source of the healing power." This was the prescription I gave him:

1. Upon waking in the morning say aloud the very first thing, "This is the day that the Lord hath made; I will rejoice and be glad in it."[2]
2. Get out of bed and take some good vigorous exercise.
3. Have breakfast with your wife and tell her that with the Lord's help it is going to be a wonderful day. Together read a chapter from Matthew, Mark, Luke, and John successively.
4. Walk, not ride, to your office.
5. Before you do any work repeat the following: "They that wait upon the Lord shall renew their strength; they shall mount up with wings as eagles; they shall run, and not be weary; and they shall walk, and not faint."[3] (Notice that the climax in this Scripture is not upthrust of spiritual power but being able to walk, i.e., keep going.)
6. At noontime take a mile walk and give thanks to God for a good morning and say aloud the Scripture verse, "In quietness and in confidence shall be your strength."[4] Keep tension down and practice having confidence that God is guiding you to right decisions.
7. Walk home after work and as you do so repeat the Bible verse, "This is the rest wherewith ye may cause the weary to rest; and this is the refreshing."[5]

2. Psalm 118:24, paraphrased   3. Isaiah 40:31   4. Isaiah 30:15
5. Isaiah 28:12

8. When you get into bed thank God that He gave you a good day. Put all the decisions you made into His hands and leave them there. Remember St. Paul's words, "Having done all, to stand."[6] Then say, "He giveth his beloved sleep."[7] And go off to sleep peacefully.

Walter T. read what I had written. "Makes sense," he commented, tucking the paper in his wallet. "I'll do it. I get what you are driving at and I'm sure it will work." It did work, I am glad to say, and indeed it proved so effective for Walter T. that he gave copies of this "prescription" to a few of his friends who seemed to need this type of spiritual treatment. He recovered his normal strength in due time and with it his temporarily lost or suspended sense of security. The improvement was not quickly achieved or in any sense miraculous. Spiritual victory only occasionally comes about in such manner, and in this case, as is usual, it was a gradual improvement marked by a few setbacks.

The mind, when in a downward spiral into negativism, tends to fight back against any attempt to reverse the process into a positive attitude. But always faith, if persevered in, proves stronger than doubt, greater than weakness. Walter T. persevered, and he did one thing which, of a certainty, added much to the directions I gave him. He became a consistent, steady, even enthusiastic Bible reader. He went on a search through the Scriptures for texts such as I had given him having to do with strength, peace, and faith. He committed these to memory and repeated them aloud daily so that the ear could hear them as the mind would think them. This man became a person of spiritual growth, and I

6. Ephesians 6:13   7. Psalm 127:2

shall forever remember him as one of the great Christians whom I have known over the years. He demonstrated the strength and the power unforgettably.

STRENGTH OVER A WEAKNESS

Throughout my ministry a question frequently asked is how can one overcome a weakness. In many cases the questioner has assumed that each person has his own particular weakness handed down to him or in some way peculiar to him, something with which he must live as best he can. Yet such persons never relinquish the hope that ultimately they may overcome or escape from the long-held weakness. Many have been quite uniformly surprised when I have suggested that they can not only overcome the weakness but actually become strongest in their weakest place.

When a weakness which dominates an individual is subjected to a major corrective effort, that very emphasis often serves to substitute a strength of greater power than the weakness it superseded. One becomes like those great people described in Scripture who "out of weakness were made strong."[8]

A workman at my farm showed me a broken metal bar. He fitted the two ends together, then subjected the joint to intense heat in the process of welding so that, as he explained, "the molecules flowed together in fusion." He told me that if he were to use a sledgehammer to hit the welded bar with force, it might break but most likely not at the point where it had been welded. He was telling me that the metal bar could become strongest at its hitherto weakest place. A similar process of

8. Hebrews 11:34

spiritual application can make a person stronger at the point of former weakness than in any other area of his nature.

While in an airport waiting room before boarding my plane, I noticed a man go to a telephone booth only a few feet away. Leaving the door open, he dialed a number, and I heard him say, "Hello, sweetheart." I concluded that he must be talking with his wife, and they carried on a conversation that was obviously heating up. After a while he apparently didn't like what "sweetheart" was saying and his words become more and more acrimonious. I was embarrassed and thought of moving to another seat farther away, but there were no others available. Finally the man let loose a stream of profanity and shouted, "Aw, skip it!" and threw the receiver so that it bounced all around inside the telephone booth. As he came out, his face was flushed (his blood pressure must have been really up) and he stomped back and forth in his fury.

Then he noticed me and apparently recognized me, for he said "Hello" and called me by name. "Did you hear that conversation?"

"How could I help it?" I replied. "You talked quite loudly."

"Well," he said, "it was my wife."

"So I gathered."

"You know, I have a wonderful wife," he added. "I really love her. But at times she is the most exasperating person in the world. I get so mad. This anger is a funny thing. I feel it all through me. It just tears at me. I get so mad!"

"How long have you been getting as mad as that?"

"Oh," he answered, "all my life. . . ."

I suppose that as a child he had tantrums. His mother

probably was a follower of the permissive theory and just let him freely express his emotional reactions. So he grew up having tantrums.

"I get mad all the time," he said. "I'm a contractor and sometimes when there is a contract to be negotiated I send somebody else to do it, because so often I make a mess of it and blow the whole thing by getting mad.

"I like to play golf," he continued, "but I don't really know why, because I get so mad. The other day I was on a par 4 hole and got onto the green in 2. I figured maybe I could get a birdie by sinking it in one putt. At least I could get a par with two putts. I was going good. Well, I putted, and what do you think that ball did? It just ran around the edge of the hole. So I had to putt again. This time the ball hung, poised, right over the hole! I could have blown it in! Do you know what I did? I got so mad that I picked up the ball, glared at it ferociously, walked over and laid it just off the edge of the green, took the putter and drove it into the earth. How in the world," he asked, "am I ever going to get over this weakness? Guess I'll just have to live with it."

"Must be pretty tough for your nice wife to have to live with it," I remarked pointedly. "Isn't it pathetic that an intelligent man should be so victimized by his emotions! You recognize that it is a weakness, do you?"

"It is my one big weakness," he answered.

"Admitting it is at least the first step toward overcoming any weakness."

"But how do I get over it?"

"Did you ever hear of Seneca?" I asked.

"No," he said. "Who is he?"

"Seneca was a philosopher in ancient Rome," I replied. "He said something about anger that would be worth its weight in gold if you could weigh a statement. He said that the greatest cure for anger is delay. When you delay, you 'cool it'; the heat goes out of it. If you had just picked up that golf ball and put it in your pocket and told yourself you would wait and get mad twenty-four hours later, you would probably have wondered by then why you ever got infuriated at the ball in the first place."

"I will try that delay tactic," he said. "I like that idea."

"But that alone will not do it," I went on. "You have a tremendous ability, my friend; you are a wonderful person and you have fine qualities, but you need to bring your emotion under control so that it will motivate for you rather than against you." I told him about the chief solution to all human problems: to put his life in Jesus' hands and let the tranquility of Jesus control and govern his mind. The technique of applying intense spiritual welding to his emotional nature was described.

"But getting free of a volatile temper isn't all that easy," he observed.

"Agreed," I said, "but neither is it all that hard once you make up your mind and draw upon the power."

I told him of a night when Ruth and I had dinner some years ago with friends in Venice at the Royal Danieli Hotel. Sitting in the moonlight in the outdoor restaurant facing the Grand Canal, we all got to talking about the power of God to change lives. One man commented that it was almost impossible for a person to change his character. Another man, a Hollywood producer, said, "I can't buy that, for I always remember with awe what happened to my father. He had the most uncontrollable temper I have ever known, and when aroused he was a terror. He would curse and swear and break things. As a boy I was frightened to death of him. When he was not angry he was a kindly man and most lovable.

"Then when he was about forty years old he was converted. He became a true Christian. He lived to be ninety years of age, and no one ever knew him to be angry again or ever to use profanity.

"I asked him once what had happened to change him so. He looked at me with those sharp eyes of his and said simply, 'Son, I met Jesus and He changed me. That's all there was to it.' And," concluded the man from Hollywood, "I have never doubted God's power since that time."

Our friend, who had been listening intently, then said in a quiet voice, "I want that to happen to me, too." And it did. People who know the man tell me that one of his chief characteristics became his control in any and all situations. He became strongest in his weakest place.

HER LIMP WAS HEALED

I related the foregoing incident to a minister in Detroit who said it reminded him of the case of a member of his church. She was a good woman, an active worker in the church and all that; but she could come into a peaceful situation and presently it was no longer peaceful. This woman had one daughter, whom she idolized. In fact, she over-idolized her. Twice the girl was on the point of getting engaged to be married, but both times her mother persuaded her out of it. "I've done everything for you," was the mother's weepy complaint, "and you shouldn't leave me to get married."

But finally the girl really fell in love. She knew it was right for her. She went to her mother and said,

"Mother, I know how you feel, but I can't help it. I love this man and I am going to marry him."

"If you do, you will put me in my grave," the mother told her.

The young woman of course did not want to put her mother in the grave, but she knew she had to go through with it or lose her own happiness. So she went to the minister and told him her story. His reply was, "I know this boy and he is O.K. If you love him, marry him—and keep on loving your mother just the same. She won't die."

So the young couple were married. But the mother would have nothing to do with her son-in-law. She hated him. Gradually she began to develop a strange limp in her left leg. She went to a doctor, had an examination, but was told that there was nothing physiologically wrong. Finally she went to her minister and asked, "Why do you suppose I have this limp?"

"I wouldn't know," he said. "Let's pray about it. And I suggest that you come to our healing services."

One day after a healing service she walked up to the minister and said, "You know, I'm a wicked woman."

The minister thought, "Now we are getting somewhere."

The woman continued, "I hate my son-in-law. I just wonder if there is any relation between that hate and this limp."

"I wouldn't know," the minister replied cautiously, "but why don't we go on the assumption that there is?"

"All right, here is what I will do. I'll go up to Grand Rapids where my daughter lives and ask my son-in-law to forgive me." She went to Grand Rapids without letting the young couple know that she was coming, went to their house, and rang the doorbell. The son-in-law came to the door. She said, "Hello, Harry. This is your evil mother-in-law. I've come to tell you that I have been acting badly. I'm here to ask you to forgive me. Will you forgive me?"

He stepped out and put his arms around her. "I not only forgive you, but I love you."

And, according to my friend the minister, they had a wonderful relationship from that moment on. Then a few weeks later the woman came walking down the aisle at church with no limp. The minister asked her, "Where is your limp?"

"It's gone," she answered, "and I feel so wonderfully different."

Now please do not infer from this incident that whenever you see anybody limping it is due to hating a son-in-law! But that was this woman's weakness, which apparently manifested itself through a weak place in her physical system. I am not a medical doctor qualified to analyze the connection, but it strongly appears that when she gave herself in love to the Lord and to the young couple she became strong where she had been weak. The positive power of Jesus Christ was manifested.

ALCOHOLISM AND CANCER OVERCOME

Arch A. was a prominent rising young man in the banking business in his area. Brilliant mentally and engaging personally, he was in line to head one of the biggest banks in the nation. Already a top vice-president, one of his responsibilities was that of entertaining important bank customers from out of town and visiting officials of other banks. As a result of the drinking often connected with such entertaining, he became thoroughly alcoholic, so much so that he would frequently appear at the bank, even in the morning, in an intoxicated condition.

He went from bad to worse in his drinking habits. The bank warned him, tried to help him, but finally had to discharge him. Due to the dissolute reputation he had acquired, he could not find a position in any other bank in the locality nor a job of any other kind. He went through his savings, and friends avoided him on the street because of his efforts to borrow money. After helping him a time or two, old associates became tired of his repeated "touches" for money. Eventually he walked the streets a kind of pariah, sliding down into the category of a common drunk and a hopeless failure. He was relieved of his chairmanship of the official board of his church and dropped from membership in the exclusive clubs where he had previously been a great favorite, a hail fellow well met. He hit bottom, and indeed so hard that if there is a lower bottom that is where he landed.

But at heart Arch A. always was a superior person, and, confused as he was, his present deplorable condition disturbed and agitated his consciouness. Therefore, he voluntarily committed himself to an institution for alcoholics. One of his jobs there was, as he tells it, "raking leaves with hobos and bums; but I was one of them, a drunk and a worthless bum." One of the hobos was a vocal atheist, and upon learning that Arch A. had been chairman of the official board of a church, said, "Mr. A., I don't believe in God and I land in this last port for drunken bums. And you do believe in God and here you are in the same place. So where is *your* religion any better than my *no* religion?" Arch A. says that this practical question disturbed his mind perhaps more than any incident that occurred in this depraved sector of his life.

Another job was that of washing dishes by hand, automatic dishwashers not having been installed. Arch A. worked at this task with other men under the supervision of a competent young woman. "Mr. A.," she said crisply, "I know that you were formerly a director of the railroad where my father is a foreman, but I want to tell you that you are the poorest dishwasher we ever had in this place. So you just get busy and wash those dishes over again until you do the job right."

Taking shower baths in the common shower room with the other male inmates, he noticed how their bodies were decorated with tattoos. But sadly he admitted to himself that his untattooed body did not mean he was any better than these defeated persons. He, too, was defeated. The treatment at the institution did not cure him other than to set him thinking. And that was something, for when one begins really to think and think deeply and honestly, as Arch A. was now doing, he is making a turn that just possibly could lead up and out of a defeatist situation.

This in-depth thinking process led to Arch's decision to return to the home of his parents in a little country village. There, daily, he took long walks and spent hours at a place where he used to go swimming as a boy. He sat whittling, a long-time habit of his, and reading my books which had previously been given him by his mother but which he had only skimmed. Now he read *The Power of Positive Thinking* with an eager intensity. Arch was by nature an outgoing positive thinker and the philosophy expressed in the book appealed to him.

He also dwelt upon the spiritual truths in the book,

the emphasis upon the Bible and upon Jesus Christ. He got the point that positive thinking really means a faith attitude and he became aware that only faith could turn his life around. Intelligently he associated faith with Christ. This thinking led him to a decision to seek the transforming grace of Christ. Arch was a religious man and knew from Christian teaching the way of salvation described in the Scriptures. But while he knew it academically, he had never applied it to himself as a person. Now he appealed to Jesus Christ to save him, and as he read and thought and prayed by "the old swimming hole" of his youth he found the Lord and the Lord found him, fully and completely. Result? He was entirely cured of alcoholism, and his joyousness knew no bounds. "Old things were passed away" and he became a "new creature."[9]

He began immediately to rehabilitate his life, and in due course, even more rapidly than the phrase "due course" seems to indicate, he was again employed in the banking business, but this time by a bank across the street from the one from which he had been discharged. Ultimately he rose to an important executive post in that bank. Relieved of alcoholism, strongly motivated by new faith and enthusiasm, his native ability reasserted itself. The business community came to hold him in high respect and esteem and seemed also to have a winsome affection and pride in him for the recovery he had made. Indeed, he became one of the most compelling demonstrations of the positive power of Jesus Christ that his city had ever known.

Then word came to me that Arch A., who had become a dear friend, had cancer. Immediately, con-

9. 2 Corinthians 5:17

cerned that this affliction might adversely affect his faith and throw him back into his old trouble, I telephoned to him in the hospital. The same old jaunty spirit came through. "Now, don't you start worrying about me," he said in a strong voice. "Just remember that we have a great Lord. Through His wonderful grace and power we licked the disease of alcoholism, and since He is still right here with me, we will lick this disease also." And he did; or perhaps we should say, they did.

Came the day when he was going all over the Southeast speaking for the Cancer Society, of which he had meanwhile become state chairman. Using his business ingenuity and innovative talent, he was persuading people everywhere to have examinations. He even created inducements in the form of a new suit of clothes for men and a new dress for ladies if they would go to be examined. He may have saved more lives than anyone in the history of prevention against cancer by his unique methods. You will perhaps not be surprised to learn that at the heart of his city, in the area where he once panhandled for handouts, an eternal light called the Arch A. light now burns day and night in his honor.

Recently at a dinner in a hotel in his hometown he was called upon to give the blessing. It was a prayer I shall never forget in which he thanked the Lord for delivering him from two diseases and concluding with "Dear Jesus, it was You who did all this for me, and remembering what I was, if You could save a man like me You can do the same for anyone who will let You take charge of his life." One thing is sure; every individual who knows Arch A. (and due to his outgoing and loving nature they number in the thousands) knows that there is an astonishing power available, and it is called the positive power of Jesus Christ. And it is revealed constantly in the experience of people who "out of weakness were made strong"[10] —like our great friend, Arch A.

HEALED BY CHANGED THINKING

In times of sickness the application of faith in the form of positive thoughts demonstrates an amazing power to heal. Many years ago Louis Pasteur developed the germ theory of disease, which signaled a historic advance in the healing process. Similarly in our time a historical breakthrough has occurred—the discovery of the importance of the thought process in the healing of disease. Back in the 1950s Dr. Smiley Blanton and I developed the American Foundation of Religion and Psychiatry. Over not a little opposition from some in both religion and psychiatry, we demonstrated successfully that religion and psychological medicine can work together as a team in correcting those unhealthy thought patterns that lead to and stimulate ill health of body, mind, and soul. We brought out the fact, now generally accepted, that many healings result when the thoughts are healed and the soul is made well.

Now we read in the press such statements as the following United Press International newspaper story headed "Positive thinking might be the best of all medicines":

> Psychologist Thomas W. Allen believes the power of positive thinking is stronger in fighting disease than all of the technology of modern medicine.
>
> Allen preaches holistic medicine—the treatment of a

10. Hebrews 11:34

patient as a whole person rather than treatment of specific symptoms of a disease. Even an illness such as cancer can sometimes be thwarted, he believes, if patients are taught to marshal their powers of mind for the attack.

"Medicine has been highly dependent on involving an outside technology in the fighting of disease," said Allen, a faculty member at Washington University in St. Louis. "Yet the resources of people have hardly even been tapped."

Most of Allen's work has been in education, where the use of imagery to achieve goals long has been successful. Now, he said, techniques such as biofeedback show that even in fighting disease, if a patient thinks in the right way, wishing may be able to make things happen.

"The use of imagery is very potent not only in helping people change their feelings, but also in changing the way the body acts. Our thoughts reverberate in our bodies. We sort of know that intuitively, but we've made an artificial distinction between our thoughts and our bodies."

The views of Allen and others have been supported by experiments. He cited one in which cancer patients taught to use imagery techniques lived longer and better lives than their doctors had thought possible.

A key point in the use of imagery to fight cancer, he said, is recognizing that cancer cells are not overpowering invaders but can be conquered.

"Patients who use imagery picture their immune system as more aggressive and the cancer cells as relatively weak and confused. That's why radiology treatment works. You bombard the body and the cancer cells are overwhelmed."

Holistic medicine requires a sharp revision of conventional attitudes toward sickness and health, Allen said.

"We've tended to believe any type of healing or sickness has to happen from the outside in," he said. "Pasteur had a hard time getting his germ theory accepted, but once it was accepted, it was made the rule for every disease."

Allen believes the theories of holistic medicine will make a big difference in the near future.

"General practitioners used to practice a type of holistic medicine—an attempt to mobilize the optimism of the individual with encouragement and personal contact. They just didn't have the tools we have now. You don't treat diseases—you treat people with diseases.

"We are so enamored of gadgets and technology that we tend to believe someone with a fancy machine can do more to heal me than I can myself."

In my own ministry I have long been aware, made so by confirmatory personal experiences, that positive thoughts have an enormous power to work creatively in the healing process. There is healing going on around us all the time. The healing of bodies, minds, and souls is a constant process.

This healing often comes about through the agency of doctors, surgeons, and nurses. Sometimes it comes through the spiritual work of ministers and priests. It has also been accomplished through the prayers and the faith of simple believers. In not a few instances it results from the joint application of scientific medicine and religious faith.

MIRACLE AT MIDNIGHT

On one occasion I was a speaker on the convention program of the American Medical Association. The vast hall in Atlantic City was filled with doctors from across the nation. Over the platform stretched a large banner with the words: "Medicine's Proclamation of Faith."

More than five thousand leading medical men applauded their association president, himself a highly respected physician, as he stressed the working relationship between religious faith and the science of medicine. They supported his further assertions that when a person is sick he should, of course, send for his doctor, but he should also send for his pastor. It was obvious that the physicians present shared their association president's belief that God is vital in the healing process, or, as a famous doctor once put it, "I treat the patient; God heals him."

In my talk at the American Medical Association meeting I told of a healing experience in which I participated some years ago as a pastor. I was serving a church in Syracuse, New York, and was awakened one night by the persistent ringing of the telephone. Snapping on the light, I noted that my bedside clock registered midnight. It was the voice of a friend and associate, a prominent doctor, that came through to me.

"I am with a patient, Mrs. _____. You know her, of course. She is very ill." He described the medical situation, stating that he had taken all the prescribed steps which the condition indicated.

"Even so," he continued, "she does not respond. While treating her medically I have also been seeking help and guidance in prayer. I feel guided to ask you to come to my patient's home and join me in applying faith to this critical situation."

This doctor, I may add, was one of the most highly respected men in his specialty, a scientist of impeccable qualifications. He was also a man of profound faith, a believer in every sense of that term.

Joining the doctor in the sickroom at about one o'clock in the morning, I found the patient in a coma, in which state she had been for many hours. The doctor suggested, "Let us try to reach her at a deep level of consciousness and stimulate in her the desire to live. This, together with the medical steps I have taken, may perhaps bring about a healing."

The doctor sat at one side of her bed, I at the other, and the nurse, who happened to be a member of my church, stood at the foot. We all prayed silently, then aloud, in turn. This was interrupted only by necessary medical and nursing procedures.

Then something extraordinary occurred. The doctor quoted several Scripture passages directed, he said, to the patient's subconscious mind. He nodded to me. "You quote some Scripture aloud." When I ceased, he resumed. Then I took it up, suddenly realizing with a start that I was quoting passages almost verbatim which I really did not know all that well. It was an astonishing phenomenon.

Then the doctor said, "I can't understand it, for Scripture is coming to my mind that I'm sure I never committed to memory." Both of us had, of course, read and heard them often.

This spiritual treatment must have continued for three or four hours. The first streaks of dawn were showing outside when suddenly the patient stirred, looked at us, and a faint smile passed over her face. She closed her eyes and began breathing normally.

"She has come out of the coma," said the doctor. "She is sleeping peacefully." He took her blood pressure and listened to her heart action. "All the signs are good," he said wonderingly, "indeed, very good."

As we stood outside the house in that dawn, my old friend was obviously deeply moved. Taking my hand, he said, "I will never forget this, nor will you." Then he added, "God has been here tonight." It was an unforgettable miracle at midnight, but it was also the application of a positive working faith.

The woman was healed and Dr. Gordon Hoople was right; I never have forgotten what happened that night nor will I ever forget him, either. Here was a doctor, and there are many of them, who knew that all medicine is God's medicine. Some of it is in the form of pills, some in liquid. Some is taken by mouth, some by injection. Some healing is by surgery. Some, by prayer, faith, and affirmation. All in a working combination.

A man who knew Dr. Hoople said, "When my time comes to die, if Doc Hoople is sitting by my bed I will know that all will be well with me in this world or the next."

Strength was supplied to this extremely ill woman from two sources: the combined faith of a Christian doctor and a pastor, and the scientific methodology of medicine. The result was that out of weakness she was made strong through the operation of the positive power invoked by two believers working as a team with Jesus Christ, the Great Physician.

HEALING POWER OF LOVE

When men and women are reduced to dire extremity, when the cares and troubles of the world overwhelm them and life appears to be just too much to endure and they tend to give way under the sheer weight of things, they can overcome if they recall the Scriptures: "In all these things we have complete victory through him who loved us! For I am certain that nothing can separate us from his love: neither death nor life; neither angels nor other heavenly rulers or powers; neither the present nor the future; neither the world above nor the world below—there is nothing in all creation that will ever be able to separate us from the love of God which is ours through Christ Jesus our Lord."[11]

I have noted in so many cases that the simple affirmation of the love of God combined with human love possesses an astonishing healing property. Just love people in the name of Christ and in His spirit, and there is released a power that within itself possesses the power to induce healing. One day in O'Hare Airport in Chicago I was waiting to board my airplane at the designated gate and was leaning against a railing watching the crowds surging along the wide hall leading to plane departure areas. I noticed a large man making his way along, and my attention was drawn to him because of his obvious attitude of weariness. His chin rested on his chest, hands hung loosely at his sides, and his feet seemed to drag. Obviously he was depressed and lacking in energy and strength.

He had a height of well over six feet had he not been stooped in despondency. Coming level with me he looked in a sidelong glance but passed me by. Then he returned and said, "Pardon me, but are you Dr. Peale?" When I told him that I was, he said, "My airplane is now boarding and I have only a moment. I am in great trouble and despair. I am completely out of strength and need help. Please say a word to me, something that will strengthen me." I sent up a quick prayer for guidance. What could I say quickly to this poor, unhappy man that would increase his strength? But when you pray, an answer always comes, and I said, "Remember, God loves you." He smiled, said, "Thank you," and

11. Romans 8:37–39, TEV

moved away. Then, nudged by God, I'm sure, I instinctively called after him, "And I love you, too." He stopped, turned around, and came back to look me full in the face. After a moment's hesitation he said, "I really believe that you do."

It was not imagination, for as he moved toward the gate for his flight he was no longer stooped in despondency, but instead picked up his feet in a sturdy stride. A long time afterward I encountered this man again at a business convention where I was the luncheon speaker. "You can never really appreciate what you did for me that day at O'Hare," he said. "You made me aware of the love of God and the love of man. I received strength in that brief encounter, and I will thank God and you as long as I live."

"Thank God, not me," I responded. "What you experienced was the curative effect of love, one of the healthiest of all emotions; or, as an old hymn puts it, 'Love lifted me.'" This case pointed up the truth that Divine-human love is indeed a strength producer, a demonstration of the positive power of Jesus Christ.

NEW PERSON EMERGES—AMAZING GRACE
The power to remake a person from weakness to strength, from failure to success, from hopelessness to creative achievement—this is the positive power of Jesus Christ in action. There is no romance, no creativity to equal it. Here we have the greatest of all human dramas—that of change from the worst to the best—and all due to spiritual power working in a human being.

One night years ago I preached a sermon in a church in downtown Atlanta as a guest of the late great Bishop Arthur J. Moore. I gave one of my usual strongly evangelistic sermons in which I promised that, by the grace of God, through faith in Jesus Christ the Savior, any person, however badly defeated, could live a great new life—one of victory, achievement, and happiness. "Whosoever will, let him take the water of life freely,"[12] and he shall be "a new creature: old things are passed away; behold, all things are become new."[13]

After the service Bishop Moore and I were in the pastor's office when an usher came and said that a "bum" wanted to see me. "I suppose he wants a handout," he commented, "although I must say he seems to have more than that on his mind. He is pretty beat-up and dirty. Do you want to see him or shall I get rid of him?"

"No; I will see him," I said. "Bring him in." The usher returned with a pretty disreputable-looking man. He appeared to be about fifty years old but volunteered the information that he was thirty years of age. At that early age it seemed that he had experienced just about everything that a down-and-out individual might have happen to him. "I listened to your sermon," he said, "and want to get it straight. You said that by faith in Jesus Christ any person—I mean any person, even a no-account character like I am—can change and have a new life, a successful and happy life. Is that what you said?"

"That is exactly what I said," I declared.

"And would that include a guy like me?"

"Absolutely it includes you."

"O.K.," he said, "I want what you promised. I believe in Jesus. I desire this new life. I am tired of being weak and a failure. I want strength and peace. What do I do now?"

"What you do now," I said, "is to pray with Bishop

12. Revelation 22:17   13. 2 Corinthians 5:17

Moore, the pastor, and me. Tell Jesus that you give yourself to Him completely; ask forgiveness for your sins. Seek the Holy Spirit. Just tell the Lord that you are a weak, broken, defeated man and throw yourself upon His Divine mercy. Then see yourself, image yourself, as a new, clean, fine person. Believe that you now, this moment, are for a fact a new man, and in our presence thank God that you are made just that by His redeeming grace."

The man did as directed and his sincerity was without doubt. After a most earnest prayer and positive spiritual affirmation he stood up before us, and even in his dirty condition the change was dramatic. His face had a light on it. He was actually transformed before our eyes. It was all so marvelously wonderful that each of us was moved to tears. It was one of the most moving and affecting incidents in my lifetime.

With dignity he shook hands with each of us and walked out into the night. With a sense of wonder we watched him depart. We were awestruck. "Strange, isn't it?" remarked Bishop Moore. "We believe in this life-changing gospel which we preach, but when we see it actually work we are astonished, and," he added, "in the last fifteen minutes we have seen the enormous power of God actually work a miracle, for that man was saved here in our presence ."

Some months passed and I was scheduled to preach in St. Petersburg, Florida, and was staying at a hotel in Clearwater. I received a message that a man who had been converted to Christ under my preaching in Atlanta wanted to see me and was in the lobby. I went down and saw a clean, splendid-looking gentleman come across the lobby holding the hands of two little girls as he walked between them. The trio made a beautiful picture, and coming behind was a lovely young woman. As they approached he began to sing an old hymn, "Amazing grace, how sweet the sound . . . " "Remember Atlanta?" he said. "How I met Jesus there? The only words for what happened to me are 'amazing grace.' May I present my wife and two daughters?"

Many years went by and I received a letter from a young woman. "I am one of the two little girls you met once in a Florida hotel with my father," she wrote. "I want to thank you for leading him to Jesus. He became an outstanding man, a wonderful husband and father. He went home to Heaven a few days ago. One of the last things he said was, 'Give my love to Dr. Peale. He led me to Christ. Tell him that my life began that night in Atlanta when I was born in Christ, and it's been wonderful all the way.'" Her letter concluded, "And I thank God and you for the loving and honorable Christian father we have had for these wonderful years. Praise the Lord!" And I, too, praise the Lord for that amazing grace.

I give thanks for the power, the wonder-working power which I have been privileged to see at work in so many lives over the years. There is nothing like it on earth, for there is no one like Him, the source of it all. May the gospel of the saving grace of the Lord Jesus penetrate the life of American society to an extent that shall truly bring in the Kingdom of God on earth. We pray that people everywhere may personally experience the joy and the peace and the victory made possible by the positive power of Jesus Christ.

As I think of the multitude of persons to whom, by God's grace, I have been privileged to bring the message, people in every walk of life, I like best, perhaps, to think of a truck driver who wrote this letter to me:

Dear Dr. Peale:

I'm a truck driver. I have just finished reading one of your sermons, which I often do sitting in my truck. They have helped me through some difficult times.

I want to thank you very much. For I truly believe with the help of the Lord Jesus all things are possible.

Thank you.

This man, on his long hauls day and night, stopping to rest awhile, reads a printed message. When he starts again down the far-stretching highway he is sustained by the positive power of Jesus Christ, who by faith rides with him all the way. And, indeed, He is with those who love Him every minute down the roadway of life and along the road that leads home.

Other Living Books Best-Sellers

74 MORE FUN AND CHALLENGING BIBLE CROSSWORDS. This brand-new batch of crosswords features both theme puzzles and general crosswords on a variety of levels, all relating to Bible facts, characters, and terms. 07-0488-6

400 CREATIVE WAYS TO SAY I LOVE YOU by Alice Chapin. Perhaps the flame of love has almost died in your marriage, or you have a good marriage that just needs a little spark. Here is a book of creative, practical ideas for the woman who wants to show the man in her life that she cares. 07-0919-5

ANSWERS by Josh McDowell and Don Stewart. In a question-and-answer format, the authors tackle sixty-five of the most-asked questions about the Bible, God, Jesus Christ, miracles, other religions, and creation. 07-0021-X

ANSWERS TO YOUR FAMILY'S FINANCIAL QUESTIONS by Larry Burkett. Questions about credit, saving, taxes, insurance, and more are answered in this handbook that shows how the Bible can guide our financial lives. 07 0025-2

THE BEST OF BIBLE TRIVIA I: KINGS, CRIMINALS, SAINTS, AND SINNERS by J. Stephen Lang. A fascinating book containing over 1,500 questions and answers about the Bible arranged topically in over 50 categories. Taken from the best-selling **Complete Book of Bible Trivia.** 07-0464-9

THE CHILD WITHIN by Mari Hanes. The author shares insights she gained from God's Word during her own pregnancy. She identifies areas of stress, offers concrete data about the birth process, and points to God's sure promises that he will gently lead those that are with young. 07-0219-0

CHRISTIANITY: THE FAITH THAT MAKES SENSE by Dennis McCallum. New and inquiring Christians will find spiritual support in this readable apologetic, which presents a clear, rational defense for Christianity to those unfamiliar with the Bible. 07-0525-4

COME BEFORE WINTER AND SHARE MY HOPE by Charles R. Swindoll. A collection of brief vignettes offering hope and the assurance that adversity and despair are temporary setbacks we can overcome! 07-0477-0

Other Living Books Best-Sellers

THE COMPLETE GUIDE TO BIBLE VERSIONS by Philip W. Comfort. A guidebook with descriptions of all the English translations and suggestions for their use. Includes the history of biblical writings. 07-1251-X

DARE TO DISCIPLINE by James Dobson. A straightforward, plainly written discussion about building and maintaining parent/child relationships based upon love, respect, authority, and ultimate loyalty to God. 07-0522-X

DR. DOBSON ANSWERS YOUR QUESTIONS by James Dobson. In this convenient reference book, renowned author Dr. James Dobson addresses heartfelt concerns on many topics, including questions on marital relationships, infant care, child discipline, home management, and others. 07-0580-7

GIVERS, TAKERS, AND OTHER KINDS OF LOVERS by Josh McDowell and Paul Lewis. Bypassing generalities about love and sex, this book answers the basics: Whatever happened to sexual freedom? Do men respond differently than women? Here are straight answers about God's plan for love and sexuality. 07-1031-2

HINDS' FEET ON HIGH PLACES by Hannah Hurnard. A classic allegory of a journey toward faith that has sold more than a million copies! 07-1429-6

HAVE YOU SEEN CANDACE? by Wilma Derksen. In this inspiring true story, Wilma Derksen recounts the hope and agony of the search for her missing daughter. Through Wilma's faith, readers will discover forgivness and love that overcome evil. 07-0377-4

THE INTIMATE MARRIAGE by R. C. Sproul. The author focuses on biblical patterns of marriage and practical ways to develop intimacy. Discussion questions included at the end of each chapter. 07-1610-8

JOHN, SON OF THUNDER by Ellen Gunderson Traylor. In this saga of adventure, romance, and discovery, travel with John—the disciple whom Jesus loved—down desert paths, through the courts of the Holy City, and to the foot of the cross as he leaves his luxury as a privileged son of Israel for the bitter hardship of his exile on Patmos. 07-1903-4

Other Living Books Best-Sellers

LIFE IS TREMENDOUS! by Charlie "Tremendous" Jones. Believing that enthusiasm makes the difference, Jones shows how anyone can be happy, involved, relevant, productive, healthy, and secure in the midst of a high-pressure, commercialized society. 07-2184-5

LORD, COULD YOU HURRY A LITTLE? by Ruth Harms Calkin. These prayer-poems from the heart of a godly woman trace the inner workings of the heart, following the rhythms of the day and seasons of the year with expectation and love. 07-3816-0

LORD, I KEEP RUNNING BACK TO YOU by Ruth Harms Calkin. In prayer-poems tinged with wonder, joy, humanness, and questioning, the author speaks for all of us who are groping and learning together what it means to be God's child. 07-3819-5

MORE THAN A CARPENTER by Josh McDowell. A hard-hitting book for people who are skeptical about Jesus' deity, his resurrection, and his claim on their lives. 07-4552-3

MOUNTAINS OF SPICES by Hannah Hurnard. Here is an allegory comparing the nine spices mentioned in the Song of Solomon to the nine fruits of the Spirit. A story of the glory of surrender by the author of **Hinds' Feet on High Places.** 07-4611-2

OUT OF THE STORM by Grace Livingston Hill. Gail finds herself afloat on an angry sea, desperately trying to keep an unconscious man from slipping away from her. 07-4778-X

QUICK TO LISTEN, SLOW TO SPEAK by Robert E. Fisher. Families are shown how to express love to one another by developing better listening skills, finding ways to disagree without arguing, and using constructive criticism. 07-5111-6

THE SECRET OF LOVING by Josh McDowell. McDowell explores the values and qualities that will help both single and married readers to be the right person for someone else. He offers a fresh perspective for evaluating and improving the reader's love life. 07-5845-5

Other Living Books Best-Sellers

STRIKE THE ORIGINAL MATCH by Charles Swindoll. Many couples ask: What do you do when the warm, passionate fire that once lit your marriage begins to wane? Here, Chuck Swindoll provides biblical steps for rekindling the fires of romance and building marital intimacy. 07-6445-5

SUCCESS! THE GLENN BLAND METHOD by Glenn Bland. The author shows how to set goals and make plans that really work. His ingredients of success include spiritual, financial, educational, and recreational balances. 07-6689-X

WHAT WIVES WISH THEIR HUSBANDS KNEW ABOUT WOMEN by James Dobson. The best-selling author of **Dare to Discipline** and **The Strong-Willed Child** brings us this vital book that speaks to the unique emotional needs and aspirations of today's woman. An immensely practical, interesting guide. 07-7896-0

WINDOW TO MY HEART by Joy Hawkins. A collection of heartfelt poems aptly expressing common emotions and thoughts that single women of any age experience. The author's vital trust in a loving God is evident throughout. 07-7977-0